Sepia Time & Blue Space

Sepia Time & Blue Space

Memoir: Archie MacAlister

Sepia Time & Blue Space
Memoir: Archie MacAlister

First published 2021
Grace Note Publications C.I.C
Grange of Locherlour
Ochtertyre, PH7 4JS
Scotland

www.gracenotepublications.co.uk
books@gracenotereading.co.uk

ISBN 978-1-913162-16-0

Typesetting by Raspberry Creative Type, Edinburgh

British Library Cataloguing-in-Publication Data
A catalogue record for this book is available from the British Library

For

Kathryn	Rosalba
Anne	Ythan
Helen	Blake
Ruaridh	Farrah
Rachel	

and for

Dorothy, whose prompting
saw that this book was made

Contents

Preface

Families everywhere who have close links to the land and the sea carry with them ancestral tales that celebrate and honour their past. The telling of tales by my family's seafaring males and their spouses was a major part of what they, like all the others, did when free from toil, some of it enriched by the songs of their people.

These oral traditions are now diminished by the scale of loss resulting from the form and pace of change that sees our worlds altered more quickly in the past 80 years than in the previous millennium. My initial interest in putting to paper some personal history was prompted by leaving notes that might give my offspring some understanding of what has been lost. The task became more complex when I had to make sense to myself of the inter-relationships of interests within a story that might interest others as it emerged.

There is of course a vanity in this, but would that my recent forebears had been so afflicted and left a more substantial record of their time, and would that I had, with foresight, prompted it.

It has occurred to me that a lifetime of writing on professional matters, the multitude of building reports and construction specifications that are part of an architect's life, might have a stultifying effect on the end product, but I would like to think that it is written much as I might have spoken it and can but hope that Oscar Wilde's comment, 'When people talk to us about others, they are usually dull. When they talk to us about themselves, they are nearly always interesting', might apply. We shall see.

The form of the narrative takes a lead from the form of my life-memory, being in two parts that are colour coded, sepia and blue, providing the book with its title.

Reminiscence

Walking up from Edinburgh's Queensferry Road, past the galleries of modern art and, dropping down to the Belfords, one is confronted by a skyline of spires, towers and domes that formed the physical backdrop to a time around 1956 that would significantly influence all my future choices.

There were earlier influences on the choices, and particularly that of the West Highland extended family, but nothing quite as seismic as the compressed dynamic of that time. It seems fitting that images of micro-geography should prompt and be at the core of a narrative that may provide a subjective note, from memory and imagination, of witness to the complex cultural riches of a lost time.

This pocket of Edinburgh could not have been more different from Glasgow, the black industrial city of endless raucous noise that I'd left. But here, a couple of miles of little river, straddled by villages and their bridges, whose names gave inklings of their origins, ran through an amazing natural topography and an equally amazing one conjured up by man – weirs and dykes, walkways and bridges through steep valley sides of woodland and garden, between villages, with occasional glimpses of the formal terraces on the tamed plateau above.

These villages on their river were quite different in character from today's middle-class enclaves. They were sturdily working class – populated by the artisans who worked in local industries, and we students stayed in and around them as itinerants, as students in Scotland's non-campus universities did. The trendy 'Baillie' in Stockbridge was then a bar of three parts – public bar (working clothes, 'spit and sawdust'), lounge bar (one might take a female) and a jug bar (for the old widow on her own), regularly visited at weekends by an advocate from Moray Place, to sip his port and lemon and discuss the world's problems with any of us with our pints or 'nips and ponies' – reminiscent of the Old Town's egalitarian intercourse some 150 years earlier. The attraction of the place still exists – the river has been cleaned up, with the demise of local industry, notably that of paper-making which was at the raw material end of the great Scottish contribution to the world's publishing, now alas all but gone.

However, the stone-defined spaces still work wonders, as romantic in their own way as that of the dramatic amphitheatre of central Edinburgh but a mile to the south. They tell a story spanning the years, from the late middle ages to the formal classic lines of Georgian architecture and Victorian engineering, seen at their best early in the year before the deciduous world obscures their definition. 'Auld Reekie' certainly reeks less, the sour fragrance of its numerous breweries is all but gone, as also is the clamour of the bells that marked church time.

This was the locale, in a Stockbridge basement flat and another along the river at Belford, in which I was introduced to a host of cultural marvels that were readily absorbed and celebrated; but my Highland grounding preceded all of that.

Ancestors

Archie Fisher's ballad 'I was born in the shadow of a shipyard crane' is an apt description of the place of my birth in Scotstoun, on the banks of the River Clyde, and the floating image of sunbeams over a railway embankment, sparkling with the minute industrial flotsam from the adjacent Stevens ship-yard, represents my earliest conscious take on these surroundings.

My mother's family had moved from the Isle of Skye to Glasgow at the outset of the First World War. It was related not just to 'opportunities' for a family of seven but to my grandfather's employment as pilot on the old *Claymore*, the MacBrayne steamer that sailed between Skye and the Clyde and was held in great affection by his family. Most of the offspring lived close to the river and were part of that Clydeside

The *Claymore* *in Oban Bay.*

Grandparents, Murdo and Marion MacLeod (c.1910).

community engaged predominantly with the yards, the sea and the Clyde Navigational Trust, otherwise known as 'the Skye Navy'. They were Gaelic speakers and their church was the Free Church of Scotland, the church of the 'anti-laird party' that fostered at least ambivalence to wealth and rank.

She met my father, a seaman from Tarbert Loch Fyne, in 1933 at that great meeting place of the Gaels – the Jamaica Street Bridge or the 'Hielanman's Umbrella', and I arrived in 1935. He was one of a family of four seamen sons and a daughter, whose mother, widowed in 1934, still lived in the family home in Tarbert, a village that has provided my bolthole since childhood. I was given

Great-grandparents, Peter and Jessie MacAlister (c.1868).

Grandparents, Archie and Margaret MacAlister (1932).

the name of my grandfather, Archibald MacAlister. It had come down in the family from the ancestor laird of that name who is happily remembered as the fellow who set up the original Tarbert Fair in 1705, which in my young days was the year's most substantial and convivial event, with a market that attracted farmers and their stock from all around, including the islands of the Southern Hebrides. I was therefore known as Archie but to my Skye grandmother I was *Gilleasbuig*, the Gaelic

Parents, Peter and Chrissie MacAlister (1934).

Christian name from which the Norman name of Archibald had been introduced in the 13th century. It was just one of many daft examples of mistranslation that occurred. *Gilleasbuig* meant something like 'the young follower of the priest who had a partially shaved head' and Archibald was an incoming name that had 'bald' to it. So, Archie it was, and not so bad to be connected to a name that brought such a time of good cheer to the village.

<hr />

Tarbert is a common enough place-name in western Scotland, as the name describes a portage where one might transport boats or goods from one navigable water to another; but this one is singular in the form of its hill enclosure, and arguably the coast's finest natural harbour, formed of an outer harbour and an inner one where the early village is located. There is a tight bottleneck between the two, and the cork in the bottle is provided by the substantial rocky *sgeir* of MacArthur's Island. It is a geography that is little tampered with, and the hills of hard metamorphic schists form a close relationship of geology and topography that leads to an exceptional sense of visual containment within the village. Perhaps it has some bearing on the equally exceptional sense of identity that has marked its inhabitants, 'the dookers', so called for their keen traditional appetite for sea birds and particularly the ducking guillemot.

The village, at the northern end of the Kintyre peninsula that was considered an island and claimed by the Vikings, controlled the portage; and in my experience, the villagers shared that psychology of islanders that presupposes their particular island being the centre of the earth and the mainland but an offshore appendage. But it had real historical significance, at least from the arrival and settlement of the Scots of Dalriada in the first millennium, when the isthmus is first mentioned. Its obvious significance is its location and the ease of access that it allowed, between the lowlands of the Clyde estuary and beyond to the western seaboard and the Hebrides. But its greatest munificence was the bounty of Loch Fyne herring which in my youth was being productively tapped by that most successful method of herring fishing, ring-netting – pioneered in Tarbert in the mid-19th century through years of legislative oppression.

The First World War, in which three of my uncles were in the trenches but survived, was in the recent past but not, however, without a legacy. My mother's brother Willie had been gassed and was unrecognisable to her when she went to meet him at Glasgow's Central Station. Like most survivors he did not talk much about it, but one thinks of the poignant tale of the Skye platoon singing the paraphrase 'I to the hills will lift mine eyes in presence of my foe', before going over the top and being cut to pieces. Another brother, Duncan, returned with a brass crucifix in his kit-bag that he had retrieved from the rubble of a destroyed church, to give to devout neighbours, a Catholic family of MacKinnons from the island of Eriskay; and I have the letter to my grandmother telling her that her son Archie, my father's eldest brother, was lost in action, only for him to have survived as a prisoner-of-war.

Only the Serbs lost more than the Scots in that conflict and the dire effect on the cultural landscape may still be gauged from the lists on every village's war memorial. However, at any reference to that war my mother would make mention of the influenza epidemic that had killed just as many world-wide; and, at this distance in time, the frenetic 1930s begin to make more sense when viewed as a reaction to the horrors and losses of these times. As a four-year-old I was about to be introduced to the second great conflagration of the 20th century.

Glasgow Backdrop

My memories of these formative childhood years are as much of Tarbert as anywhere else, but the earliest clear recollection is of a visit to the great International Exhibition of 1938 in Bellahouston Park and being swung between my mother and her sister Ina as we walked along the Paisley Road. I recall the whiteness of the buildings, and perhaps it was Thomas Tait the architect's modern centrepiece which marked the memory. Shortly after this, and just before the outbreak of the Second World War, we moved away from the Clyde to a small council housing development of two-storey houses at the very edge of the City's northern boundary; and it was here that youthful memories really kick in.

At a stretch it might be considered as a garden suburb, and our garden was but 100 yards from farmland which stretched for 15 miles to the Campsie Hills. This farmland and the streets of the suburb were our playground and, although city boys, we were familiar with the wild life of hedgerow and pond and the wonders of seasonal change. This idyll, and it was such in relation to the Glasgow slums which neighboured it to the south, was all but engulfed by the demise of local industry and massive post-war housing developments which had as little to recommend them as the Stalinist equivalents being built at the same time in Central Europe, although the latter might boast an opera house.

The local industry of that time included MacFarlane's Saracen Foundry and St Rollox Engine Yards. I saw something of the latter's significance in the scale of the steel monsters, Pacific

Class engines, that emerged from these Springburn works and the invention required in getting them from that plateau to the Clyde and thence to the continents of the world. A deep steel girder bridge spanned the steep downhill road and a local worthy had painted in huge letters, in the web of the beam, the dismissive *Poch mo Thon.* Not so many years since, the great John MacLean and associates had caused Westminster to ring George Square with troops and tanks; and when Hamish Henderson wrote his anthem 'Freedom come all ye', with its line 'when MacLean meets with his frien's in Springburn', did he know of that girder bridge? Whatever – Gaels were to be found outwith Partick and the Skye Navigational Trust. While the MacFarlane foundry's significance was less obvious, apart from the endless racket, I found myself years later working in a studio overlooking the Gulf of Guinea where the MacFarlane brand name was cast in the iron structure that sheltered me from the equatorial sun and rain – parochial we were not and I liked the old surname that was shared with my Tarbert gran and Neil Munro's *Para Handy*.

Highland Interludes

The primary school that served our community was dedicated to the three R's and run by a stern Miss Cameron of whom all we infants were in awe. She was a native of Mull, who occasionally passed the time of day in the street with my mother or grandmother in their native Gaelic. With the outbreak of war the year before I became a 'scholar', the title with which my maternal grandmother invested me, and in the expectation of early German air-raids, my mother, eight months pregnant, decamped with me to her sister Maryann in Broadford on the Isle of Skye, where she gave birth to a daughter on the 4th November – quite an occasion for a four-year-old as well as the mother, as I was in the same Tilley lamp-lit room and only missed the detail of this great event by the local doctor placing a blanket over my cot. There in my quiet dark I could hear my mother's rather dramatic calls, with my father's name popping up, in a kindly yet anguished way, during the proceedings, as my new sister Mona MacKinnon MacAlister arrived. The following day, and for the remainder of our stay in this lovely household, the butcher's van arrived and we all had beef tea – good stuff for a nursing mother and just grand for the four-year-old who, with his box of miniature tools, had found employment with the road gang repairing a little bridge outside our door; and it is difficult to think how I was not a goddamn nuisance to these tolerant fellows. This was still a Gaelic world and would that I had had as much care for the language as I had for my box of tools. But when not thus employed, my cousin Duncan, the elder son of the house, carried me about on his shoulders as we wandered the shore. He went on to become a chief engineer at sea and, in retirement in Australia, was to the fore in the setting up of Sydney's Gaelic radio service, while vociferously decrying all his cousins who didn't have 'the Language of Eden', and Scotland in general for its notorious political cringe! Would that he had lived to see the advent of the Scottish Parliament, an idea that he promoted to the end.

So the budding 'scholar' returned to the city and duly started school, but only for a week before being struck by diphtheria – one of the lethal hazards of the day. Extreme temperature suited the red-raw fire-lit room from which I departed to the fever hospital at Ruchill, where eventual recovery from the choking suffocation of this killer followed, although the other little unfortunate from the class succumbed. I have pleasant memories of the six-week hospital stay – good soup and egg sandwiches, escaping the rationing, seemed to be the order of the day. My father's brother Tom, back from sea, arrived with a red fire engine for my Christmas, while real theatre was provided by German air-raids when the ack-ack opened up and we little ones were transported to the basement, there to be suspended vertically in leather harnesses on the walls while nurses sang to us during the uproar in the skies. Surprisingly I remember no uproar from us but only the accompanying excitement.

And the 'scholar' was not yet going back to school, as his *Sgiathanach* grandmother, his great friend, decided that *Gilleasbuig* could do with some mountain air after his ordeal, so off we went into Highland Perthshire where her brother Kenny *Mór* was head shepherd and general factotum at the head of Glen Lochay. He met us with pony and trap at Killin and in early Spring sunshine we jogged up the glen to Kennock, to the substantial farmhouse, bothy and barn.

There my grandmother and I shared a bedroom where the early sun arrived each morning, or so it seemed, and I rose to start the day by pouring water from a substantial ceramic pitcher into a matching bowl with which my gran could refresh herself and then down to the kitchen where Kenny's wife served our brose, scones and tea. Although it was still the crack of dawn we were the last for breakfast as the shepherds from the bothy, about a dozen of them who were all either Gaelic or Welsh speakers, had long gone to the hill.

There was a war on, but I cannot recall having any care or concern but to get out to explore the flat granite slabs with the puzzle of the patterns of small neat holes that bounded the fast-flowing Lochay, or to dig miniature shelters in the deep pine needles of the adjacent conifer plantation, and have a chat with the cattle in the warmth of the byre while rummaging about in their large grain bunker for the lumps of sweet malt that were my treat.

The cheerful sociability that was shared by all in front of the large black stove at the end of the day was another, as I was dandled on the knees of giant shepherds who found great amusement in my tales of the day's adventures and my 'shooting' with my six-gun and bringing home a rabbit that I had actually retrieved from a snare. Now the bothy, the barn, the conifers, the Gaels and their Welsh colleagues are gone and only a silent farmhouse and the granite slabs with their holes remain to remind me of these times, but 'so it goes' as Vonnegut would have it. A rather more cheerful reminder occurred when I met Dougie MacDonald 50 years later, who could share such memories as his father had been the gamekeeper in Glen Lyon, over the hill from Lochay, and a great friend of Kenny *Mór* with whom he had shared earlier experience in the trenches of the First World War and on Rhum in their congruent careers.

The significance that such interludes may have in one's stable early years might be found in a psychiatrist's chair, but they clearly form a reservoir of robust reference for all time. A memory of that pine plantation and the perfume of its resin and needles re-emerges with every visit to a coniferous forest, just as other sensory exotica such as the first sip of a Highland malt sharply brings back the introduction to the wonders of that marvellous liquor when it was delivered as the Highland placebo to the pain of infancy's toothache. Here we obviously had a head start on our European comrades – with their grapa, marc and vodka – in our appreciation of fine quality refreshment.

Second World War

While rural 'interludes' continued, formal primary education happened back in the city under the firm but benign regime of Miss Cameron. All the teachers were female and this exposure to the fair sex was furthered by the home-life experience where only sporadically did father or uncles appear for a couple of days' leave from their duties in the Atlantic.

But when I was not kicking a ball about with my pals, or cycling to the Campsie Hills, it was drawing which gained my attention. Neither at home nor at school was it encouraged or discouraged, nor was it from the world around me that I drew but from sources such as *War Illustrated*, to which our household subscribed, and a botanical encyclopaedia gifted to me by an old neighbour. The former carried detailed line graphics of tanks and ships and planes that provided the imagery to accompany the ever-present BBC war news of the years when I went from age four to ten – the ditty 'Lillibullero' introduced the news which had, as I remember, the title 'Into Battle'. What a time to be a boy; and it was all as interesting as the coloured geometry of the images in my precious kaleidoscope.

This was particularly true if one's family survived the blitz and one's father and uncles the sinkings, some repeatedly in convoy duties in the Mediterranean and the North Atlantic. We regularly rushed, in the middle of the night at the air-raid siren's baleful whine, to the garden shelter, and invariably my mother the last, as she had to find the small Gladstone bag in which she kept the insurance policies that would see us all buried properly if the worst came to the worst. We would occasionally hazard a peek out at the night sky, where searchlight beams stretching to infinity would catch the silver of barrage balloons, a quite incongruous but attractive image belying the clamour of the ack-ack shell fire – was there ever a better example of onomatopoeia. But then the 'all clear' siren would bring the curtain down on this drama, allowing us to safely return to bed, with the promise of morning excitement in the litter of ack-ack shrapnel that we boys collected and exchanged after every raid. There were other scares – the unexploded landmine some yards from my father's sister's substantial house in Anniesland. But at the age of eight, when I might be staying with her, I was more terrified of a jelly bag, stained red by regular autumnal use, that hung on a cane on the half-landing of the stair, than any of the regular action that centred on the nearby River Clyde. What could that have been about?

Quite early in the war I went with my father's brother Tom to Tarbert, by road over 'the Rest and Be Thankful' into Argyll; and there, camped under canvas in the snow at Glen Kinglas, was a large part of the Polish army that had escaped via Persia and were in training to join forces with our 8th Army in the push after El Alamein. It was an introduction to the reality of the multinational alliance against the Nazis and I saw much more of this as the war progressed, with my father bringing Free Dutch and Free Norwegian sailors, and eventually Americans, home to our simple hospitality.

The most frightening event was the arrival of a telegram as, in these days before phones in every household, such a communication would normally inform of combatants 'killed' or 'missing in action', and my mother's brother Alex had a particular propensity for raising such scares by being sunk and posted missing on more than one occasion: all of which he survived, but the last one in 1943 was a close call. The

SS *Rhexenor* was out of West Africa on passage to New Brunswick when she was hit by two torpedoes in mid-Atlantic. Alex spent 21 days adrift on a lifeboat, when, having covered 1236 miles, he was picked up by a US merchant vessel then taken to St Thomas in the US Virgin Islands. A week's recuperation, then shuttled by mail boat to Havana, where the 16 survivors were given a special send-off dinner in a fancy hotel. He was sitting next to a fellow seaman, Colin, from the Island of Harris, blethering in Gaelic, and from across the table a gentleman came around and sat between them, explaining that he was the head of the Canadian Bank in Havana whose first language was Gaelic and whose father had been the banker in Portree on the Isle of Skye. Alex remembered him and the threesome ended the evening over a bottle of Scotch, before getting back across the Atlantic on a tanker out of Baltimore. He always thought of himself as lucky, as also do I in having him as an uncle. My mother, although regularly exasperated by his bonhomie and his drinking when ashore, might from time to time receive a few pound notes in an envelope with the note, 'Dear Chrissie, Buy yourself a hat'. That was his style. He endeared himself to me when, at the age of ten, he took me along to see the world boxing flyweight champion Jackie Paterson train before a title fight. He also introduced me to a snooker hall one wet Sabbath with the advice, 'Keep your thon (arse) down and your eye along the cue', while the expected divine retribution for such impropriety on the Lord's Day passed me by.

But still on the matter of telegrams – a crazy aunt, one of my mother's lovely sisters who could afford such an expensive form of communication (about a shilling at that time) would use them to inform family of totally unimportant happenings while frightening the wits out of the recipient – one such comes to mind, 'Archie arriving today with Tony' (1944), on my taking the train from Oban to Glasgow with the gift of a tame rabbit! I can cheerfully reminisce now about telegrams but recall thinking at the time that I should hide below the table, while Iain Crichton Smith's short story 'The Telegram', really catches the terror of such an event.

The short shore leave of any of the menfolk was, of course, celebrated and they would huddle around the radio transcribing morse code, with which all of them were conversant, and little scraps of information would be gleaned about movements at sea. Some small mementos of actions, like a German pilot's wings, would come my way but better than that was to be taken down to the Clyde at Bowling, where my father's ship the *Iris*, a cable-layer, was alongside. Many merchant seamen like my father were transferred into the Royal Navy, talked of in these days as the Senior Service – well, 'senior' enough to be the only one to have the great rarity of WHITE bread – but to be in the company of these men in the spick and span warmth of a freshly painted ship, and being strapped into and spun in an Oerliken gun pointed to the skies on the forward deck, allowed me some kudos in the blethers with my school pals the following day, to which 'white' bread and some empty brass shells gave credence.

A shipmate of my father on the *Iris*, Ian Nicolson, was a cousin of my mother and also from Skye. In 1944 they had a spell of some months in Funchal in Madeira, where in the peace of its harbour they worked on the preparation of deep-sea cables, a time that both considered the best experience of their war years. Seamen of that generation were craftsmen and appeared to me to be able to do anything – one of them even soled my boots – but Ian's accomplishment was special. In that period he built a detailed scale model of the *Iris* and the skipper offered him £100 for it, probably as much as he would have earned in some months, but he declined the offer. At war's end and demobbed, he moved with his wife to the hamlet of Inverasdale on Loch Ewe where she was the teacher and there they raised a family. The classic model ended up in their boys' bath and Ian, in the school playground, built a 30-foot sea-going craft from the stem up while his son, a few years later, was to become a naval architect.

Sundays

The greatest misery for me, although I have little in the way of miseries with which to compare it, was the loss of one day every week to strict observance of the Sabbath. This deluded nonsense in our home was due to the aforementioned grandmother who had brought all of her Skye ways with her to the city and, as she stayed much of the time with us, my dear mother, well tutored in such matters, dutifully saw that we offspring were introduced to the faith of our fathers – the hell-fire variety. Certainly, before I was much older, I was questioning how such kindly, intelligent people could choose to shut down 14.28% of their waking hours. Three-hour-long church sermons dealing with the obscure theology of the Old Testament were excruciating for the lively young or for the lively old – my father, back from the serious matter of life or death in the North Atlantic and press-ganged into attendance, would occasionally nod off, only to receive an elbow in his ribs from mother. I should not know what varnish tastes like but I do, and it must date from my being but three feet tall or the height of the bible shelf of the forward pew! At least in school when blanket boredom struck, one could surreptitiously carve one's desk, but what retribution from the heavens at the very thought of such, in this weird place. The minister himself, by all accounts, was a reasonable fellow when clear of the pulpit, yet how could he fill his days dreaming up new ways to convince us of our sins? I regularly pass the south side of Dean Parish Church and below the chiselled *Nec Tamen Consumebatur* in the sandstone wall a deciduous bush has been planted which bursts into autumn flame each year and, that I comprehend its significance, reminds me of the Jesuits' 'Give me the child until he is eight...'

The temper of our family, outwith this day of rest, seemed little affected by the harshness of the pulpit's misery but I can think of minor *schadenfreude* occasions and less-than-Christian goodwill at the transgression of some whom Burns could have had in mind when penning 'Holy Willie's Prayer'.

Some compensation for the loss of my Sundays preceded them when on Saturdays I assisted my grandmother, a consummate baker, in the making of the following week's bread and the piles of oatcakes and scones that would feed our very own multitude in the following week. But if there was a redeeming feature to the bleak Sundays, it would have to be the congregation's unaccompanied singing of the Psalms of David, where a precentor would introduce each line of the psalm in advance of the congregation. John Purser writes in *Scotland's Music* of the 'uncanny emotional charge which such singing produces', and it still has the power to raise the hairs on the back of my neck. It is 'singing where each individual has a certain freedom of tempo and embellishment so that the tune is heard slightly out of phase with itself and, as it were, in different colours simultaneously. This too is part of a tradition as old as Christianity, with its nearest parallels in the Middle East...retaining a style of singing with roots in very ancient Christian chant'. Although now it is mainly confined to the Hebrides, my early experience of it was in a city church, fervently sung by a congregation of many hundreds, and the common analogy to the repetitive rhythm – that of waves breaking on a shore, with a fine swell running – is apt, but the Australian/Scottish poet Les Murray's *The Gaelic Long Tunes* really does it justice in lines like these:

In disdain of all theatrics, they raised straight ahead,
From plank rows, their beatless God-paean, their
giving like enduring.
And in rise and undulation, in Earth-conquest mourned
as loss
all tragedy drowned, and that weird music impelled them,
singing, like solar wind.

All of Scotland fell silent on the Sunday, although not to the extent of our household and, outwith the Bible's strictures, a day of rest was certainly called for, particularly after the home-grown conviviality of the preceding Saturday night. Neighbours and family would arrive at our fireside and the tradition of the ceilidh house and the informal evening of song and story survived in the city. My mother's brother Duncan, with his rough untutored baritone, was a star who gave us the great Skye songs of love and loss, while from the top pocket of his navy-blue suit he would twirl a handkerchief into a tight little rope, the end of which would be offered to a female in the company, gently to be swung to the tempo of the melody. Out would come the gramophone and from my mother's collection of records Archie Grant, *Mòd* medallist and old friend, would get an airing or perhaps, quaintly, some Hawaian guitar music, before the women would break into rousing '*port à beul*'. Everyone contributed, and the repetitive nature of much of it was of no significance as the story or song was invariably given a twist to suit the mood or form a link with that of the previous performer. What visiting guests, a US seaman in 1944 for instance, made of all this I can but guess, but that open-door policy has followed me around over the years and sometimes with results as exotic as the Hawaian connection. In 1980 I met an American Indian when out for a beer in Edinburgh city centre. Pablo could have been a model for a totemic sculpture from the rainforests of British Columbia, but he was a plains Indian and a librarian in El Paso University, where he was also working on a PhD on Pablo Neruda, the poet promoter of peace among men, and for whom I shared enthusiasm. He came home with me to share a dram and a family meal and I saw him off on the midnight train to London thinking that would be the end of the brief but lively encounter, but a few weeks later three boxes arrived, each with a different stoneware dove of peace, *à la* Pablo Picasso – a trinity of Pablos!

But those quiet Sundays also saw a break from our running wild, and provided the time spent with the magical exposition of coloured geometry thrown in the triangular section of my kaleidoscope and the collection of old spectacle lenses which, when not entertaining budding arsonists in Summer, were used in endless unsuccessful attempts to project torch-lit images which I had scratched on blank film retrieved from a burnt-out US army supply train – the notion of primitive film technology was there, but hardly the tools. And the continuing fascination with drawing and its implementation – pens, paper, pencils, none of which were plentiful in these war years – moved along. I can only surmise that it was simply the crafted ability of drawing or reproducing an image that I was chasing – some way from the study or questioning of the visible or its use in the communication of ideas, but gradually it moved into these realms. It was certainly linked to the curiosity engendered by maps and postage stamps. Hours were spent drawing maps of the Treasure Island sort, with hints of locales, that I knew or dreamt of, while the copying of atlas maps coloured up to denote rainforest or desert was helped along by the postage stamp images of exotic places from my seafaring uncles. To this imagined magic came some real treasures from the same fellows – a little sachet of shark's teeth, another of moonstones, a compass, a watch; and all of them with stories – of who had been taken by the shark, or of the 'bum-boat' from which the watch was bartered. Years were to pass before I saw how these youthful efforts were in spirit and content closer to the story maps of antiquity than to the grid maps of my schooling, and it was Tarbert experience that gave substance to it.

The Village

Map of Tarbert, 1887.

Tarbert had been a place of settlement since earliest times, and its significance in the medieval age is recorded in the scale of the ruins of the fortifications that sit in a controlling position above the isthmus. They bear witness to Scotland's wars of independence and the fluctuating power of Clan Donald's lordship of the western seaboard, in which my ancestors had some interest; but the village as we know it only came into being shortly after 1811 when Thomas Telford's breast-wall defined and delineated a harbour suitable for the emerging herring industry and provided the solid geometry of the building line of Front Street. The village was fortunate in that the local lairds were not of that notoriously avaricious breed who were party to the Clearances after the disaster of the final Jacobite rising, and Culloden. In fact, they promoted the interests of the herring industry with development of the harbour and its quays, although their position of authority could lead them into strange vanities – like the formation of a mountain battery from a village of seamen, who marched out of the village in 1914, to see from Gallipoli's heights an allied landing fleet that could not handle inshore boats being blown apart by Turkish guns.

Tarbert, with Loch Fyne skiffs at the quay.
The white gable of Argyll House may be seen behind the horse standing on
the quay. (Photographer unknown).

Close to the western end of the oval inner harbour and the centre of the village was the family home of my grandparents from 1905, where my father, his three brothers and a sister were reared. Known as Argyll House, it had been an inn during the previous century and was what would now be considered a double-upper flat above commercial property; but such vocabulary is thin indeed in telling anything of the character of a property which simply reeked of earlier times and made a great impression on this youngster.

Three families shared Argyll House. The McCalliens – Ned the shoe- and boot-maker, his wife and his brother William, the very able painter of Tarbert fishing life – occupied the ground floor, below our family home; while the MacMillans made quality leather footwear, as well as sea-boots and 'fraochans' for the hill, at the east end of the block. We small boys found sanctuary from wild weather in the Argyll's shared access

Argyll House early 1900s.

Myself, aged seven, on the slip opposite Argyll House. Tie and shoes suggest it was a Sunday and I was going to the kirk.

and pipe-clayed stairwell while watching Ned in awe as he, with a mouthful of segs, unerringly in rapid-fire nailed soles to boots. Along with the 17th-century cottages in the back street, the Argyll was to vanish and be replaced by sterile 1960s development that bears little relation to the scale or forms that made up the early village street – alas, the way of the world!

Our house was accessed from the front street by a stone spiral stair to a little hall overlooking the harbour and from a timber spiral stair at the rear rising from the kitchen yard to a landing with a very large Belfast sink – the formal and the informal. From the front hall there was a parlour that was impeccably Victorian: embossed wallpaper, mahogany furnishings with horsehair upholstery that caught one behind the knees, and a marble and slate fireplace with statuettes that had been won by the men of the house at shooting competitions. Full silver service was the order of the day for weekend meals in this room and we even had bone napkin holders, but along a dark corridor there was the rear landing and its Belfast sink where the seamen father and sons would have slunged down and washed off the herring scales before going through to the kitchen with its large black range. As a teenager, I followed this pattern when I spent my summers on Archie McCaig's skiff, the *Seonaid*, some 30 years later.

The darkest room in the house was the kitchen, sparsely lit by a little window over the 'jaw-box' sink but cheered by the red glow and the welcome cooking odours of the iron range. Occasional visitors might appear in the morning in this informal setting over cups of tea, and I think particularly of an older lady, draped in cloth and bringing with her the scent of the weather and wood fires. She was a Townsley, the family of travelling people who lived in an encampment of bentwood tents just above high-water tides at the head of West Loch Tarbert. They were indigenous Scots and an intrinsic part of village life of whom I never heard a disparaging word, although that could not be said of her husband Jock Townsley's playing of the pipes. They wandered about the village and the local roads with their cart, following odd-job employment, and travelled very little from their base, unlike other travelling families in the Highlands who were renowned for their knowledge of pearl-fishing or tin-smithing, as well as being the custodians of an astonishing wealth of traditional stories and songs.

I would have been about nine when responsibility for the maintenance of the paraffin lamps fell to me, with the trimming of the wicks and the cleaning of the elegant glass chimneys and bowls. This was an important task, as the tortuous internal layout could be difficult to follow in the gloom of an overcast day, and I took it seriously. The smallest, a 'night light', lit the stone entrance spiral stair and the lamp forms became more elaborate, from that of simple utility in the kitchen to the grandeur of the parlour, while my little sister and her equally uncertain brother went warily about, as who knew what might lurk in the corners of this ancient place and in the shadows beyond the modest radius of the flickering light?

It is not possible to consider Tarbert without some understanding of the significance of Loch Fyne herring, on which the village was dependent and which had long enjoyed the reputation of being the finest and most delicate of the species. They were a staple of our family's diet, plump and fresh – fried in oatmeal in the summer and autumn months and then in their salted form, from the pantry's firkin, throughout the winter. No-one seemed to tire of them, although, in wishful thinking, they could be referred to as two-eyed steak. Across the North Channel, where herring were traditional Lenten fare, the praise of our Irish cousins could be qualified, used as they were to fasting and deprivation. The anonymous author of this spirited 16th-century poem, from the Irish Gaelic, champions the fish with just a hint of a sting in its tail:

Hail to your coming, O Herring

Hail to your coming, O Herring;
draw near, my precious one:
Good health ! A hundred welcomes
Indeed you deserve a big 'Failte'.

By my father's hand, I tell you, herring,
no matter, how good are Boyne salmon
it is for you that I fashioned this poem
most noble and most youthful one.

Good sir, whose glittering body
makes no false promise,
a friend like you I never had;
may nothing trifling separate us.

Let the sages of Banba reflect on
who is best of this trinity;
herring is best of all fish
including salmon and pike.

Herring, sweet tempered and merry,
our mainstay during Lent,
favourite son of my friend,
to me you were long in coming

Though many of your kin
fell into my plate last year, do not
dwell on it in anger or resentment,
you who are the friend of the poets

Herring, salty and cheerful
who is never closed off or surly
to me your coming is never unpleasant,
in you my eye sees a friend

As miserable Lent begins, Good Sir,
who is our drinking companion
– til Easter comes –
great is my respect for you

(English translation, Malachi McCormick)

Tarbert had been at the centre of the development of ring-netting, and Angus Martin wrote of the fishermen and this fishing technique: 'Herring fishermen were the elite of the class, and ring-netting the most sophisticated of the methods worked in British waters. With ring-netting, a degree of science – hitherto unrealised – entered the practice of catching herring'.

However, ill-considered and unworkable legislation to restrict herring fishing to the less efficient method of drift-netting was enacted in 1852 and there followed periods of great deprivation and serious violence in the resistance by the Tarbert fishing community. Its repeal in 1867 coincided with the arrival of herring steamers which took fish directly from the fleet at sea to the same day's morning market in Glasgow – a huge stimulus to the fresh fish trade and the village's commercial life.

The physical shape of the place had been remodelled with Telford's new harbour, fit for ring-net fishing skiffs and the steamers that served them; the introduction of modern ways and capitalist enterprise was afoot and it was into this 'new' village that my grandparents were born. A social and cultural change had also taken place with substantial migration from the Lowlands. In my youth I thought that this migration was the reason for the demise of Gaelic, but this was not the case, as the Lowlanders were soon assimilated into the old Gaelic society and they themselves became Gaelic speakers. But it would not be for long, as the language was about to come close to extinction. Regular daily steamers, arriving from the Clyde's urban centres, were instrumental in Tarbert's new-found popularity as a holiday resort. English became the currency of communication; concurrent with the employment of monoglot English-speaking teachers in the village school and the repression of the use of Gaelic in the playground. This was the scenario in which John MacDougall Hay set his epic novel *Gillespie*, where his depiction of character within the harsh new inter-relationships of Calvinism and capitalism was not to the taste of many in the Victorian village, an aversion that has persisted until this day.

The project of 'improvement' begun by Tarbert lairds in the late 18th century fully subscribed to the concept of progress that would speed the severance of the cultural links with the past. From family experience, there was no complaint about the 'improvement' into which the populace at large had bought, but the Gaelic language was to disappear, just as the herring would a hundred years later.

Although both my grandparents came from a fishing and tacksman background, the Gaelic cultural loss would by all accounts more likely have been felt by my grandfather and his sons, who had a greater empathy with the oral history and deeds of the ancestors than my grandmother, the village postmistress, very much at home with the new world of the laird and the banker, although still very much part of the village life that was inclusive of Townsley travelling folk. My mother told the story of meeting her future parents-in-law for the first time in the early

1930s when her husband-to-be was on the high seas and she took the steamer to Tarbert to be met at the pier by my *seanair* (grandfather). She was impressed by this old fellow, a 'handsome Highland gentleman in his navy serge suit' who, taking her bag, suggested that as the summer day was fine they should walk the mile into the village, while he told her of his fondness for the island of her birth and its people, with whom he had many friendly dealings in his sojourns to the 'north herring fishing'. Arriving in the sunlit village on a Saturday around noon, and knowing nothing of the life of a fishing community, she thought it strange that such a large body of men should be sitting at their ease, smoking and chatting with legs dangling over the sea wall, not realising that they awaited a shave in the old weigh-house, which also sat on that wall and accommodated the barber; the first stage of the Saturday's social ritual that would move onto the village's public houses for the 'sharing' of the week's financial return for their endeavours.

Her relationship with my *seanair* flourished till his death, and although that with my grandmother was friendly there was little of the warmth that she expressed in all references to the old fellow. Perhaps I should qualify this view, as she had nothing but good to say of all the familial males, while in the immediacy of the family the occasional comment about my grandmother's cooking or the 'affectation' of bone napkin-holders would out and this difference could probably be explained by her sharing with my grandfather something of that sensibility of the ancient web of culture and tradition of the Gael, the *duthchas*.

But such sober musings can have me reaching for my well-turned pages of Flann O'Brien's satire of Gaeldom, *The Poor Mouth*, and how he would have related to the realities of the Tarbert portrayed by the writer 'Gowrie' in 1867 – the actual scene of a ceilidh in a fisherman's cottage, drams and songs and the old head of the house dancing a sword dance to music produced by a three-string fiddle while a pig lay cosy in a barrel by the fire. And 'Terpsichore in Tarbert', as Gowrie had it, continues 120 years later – the pig in the barrel has gone but there are drams and a late evening of songs with fiddle and accordion accompaniment. A knock on the door finds a young man in his 30s who is barely known to us – 'I'm just off the Islay ferry and this is the only light in the village', he says in response to our queries. He contributes songs in Gaelic, singing with a range and ability that the angels might envy. He is from South Uist and wears a knitted navy-blue gansey that is textured with patterned symbols that intrigue our French guest. He explains that it was knitted by his grandmother and these subtle symbols tell something of his life and ancestry. It also interested me, and the following day my mother had a telephone conversation in Gaelic about such knitting tradition with an old lady on the island of Eriskay, which resulted in one of my daughters leaving for foreign parts with the gift of a gansey that referenced some of her connections, and so it goes.

The Victorian parlour and the Belfast sink seem to me to express rather well the dichotomy of the old Argyll House, while the books which were to be found at that time in old timber trunks in the attic rooms, school prizes dating from a time before the First World War, were all of a type celebrating Victorian exploration and imperial power, the exploits of the Scotts and Shackletons and the opening up of the great Canadian wilderness or *The History of the Highland Regiments*, which, of course, gave no hint of Wolfe's cynical 'No Great Mischief' on the heroic Highland losses at the taking of Quebec.

The two attic rooms were my favourite spaces. They were light and airy and almost empty as their use as bedrooms by the sons of the house in other days was gone. But the spaces felt well-used and my father, on being asked when he had started smoking, told me that he must have been about nine. With his brother Tom he had got hold of some 'shag tobacco' and they had rolled a smoke in the fine paper of an old bible, blowing the smoke directly up the attic's chimney. They appear to have missed out on the 'God-fearing' bit of their time.

But as the war moved towards a close, I was running with my peers and the quay was our hub. There were mountains of fish boxes with which to form tunnels and shelters or we would scramble about below the timber quay at low tide on the slippery seaweed-covered frame while netting saithe, and of course there were boats. At this time there were always three or four air-safety launches and occasionally a motor-torpedo boat at the quay, and the sailors were quite relaxed about our presence. They had a chocolate ration which they would share with us and we might help with small tasks, as on one occasion when I was in a fo'c's'le having a mug of tea and there was discussion which I did not comprehend among the band of seamen. Eventually I was asked to go to the chemist for an errand. Well, I nipped ashore to the Medical Hall and asked Isobel for a packet of 'French letters' and was given a clip on the ear and told that she was immediately going to report me to my grandmother, which of course she never did; but one grew up quite quickly in such circumstance, while a sense of humour about matters sexual developed with the years; like the old, long-retired fisherman visiting the same establishment and asking for a gross of this product only to be asked by the lady behind the counter what he could possibly do with such an order and he quietly replied 'Well, Ah just love the smell o' burnin rubber'.

Barmore

Just a mile north of the village there is another deep embayment where the peninsula with the misnomer Barmore Island forms bays to the north and the south. It is part of an estate earlier known as Barmore (Large Ridge) but, on its being sold by the MacAlister laird to Campbells in 1747, the name was changed to Stonefield, derived from the Gaelic Achnacloich on Loch Etive, whence they came.

Map of Barmore, 1887. The loop of the stone fish trap may be seen in South Bay, known to us as the Bagh mu Dheas.

Both bays have boulder and shingle shores between high- and low-water mark, but the southern one, the *Bagh mu Dheas* (South Bay), is then of fine sand where an old stone fish trap forms a loop at low-water mark, inside some rocky *sgeirans* (skerries) that provide partial shelter to the bay's exposure. There, a few yards from the shore on the landward side, sits a cottage, below the steeply rising rock face of Barr Hill that is almost engulfed in a lush evergreen woodland, where I spent some magical summers with my father's cousin, her husband and two sons.

The remains of the fish trap on the sand and the cottage on the shore.

This woodland was contiguous with the great 'wild' garden, created by the botanist Sir J D Hooker in the mid-1800s, and, 'Here more so than in any other garden that I know, is a reminder of the Himalayan scene' was the head gardener David Hannah's description a hundred years later. Rhododendrons, azaleas and hydrangeas grew in some profusion and great luxuriance, keeping company with mighty conifers and indigenous hardwoods by the gorge of the Barmore Burn. The perfumes and colours of that world have joined the sensory exotica of childhood, as I recall the early evenings and the trip along the gorge side to collect fresh milk with my zinc pail at the home farm.

Heralding the awakening day were the calls of the shore birds – the oyster-catcher's shrill repetitive call and the evocative *Pill-il-il-iu* of the redshank, used in the *caoine* (the cries of mourners associated with funerals), 'keen' in English, since Gaelic's early Christian centuries – and as there is barely a memory of rain or storm, although the burn was regularly in spate, the eastern sun soon filled the *Bagh mu Dheas* with warm summer light and after porridge it was down to the shore and the old green *punt* – the Tarbert boys' sole word for a rowing boat.

Scrambling about in the rock crevices and gullies, the little green shore crabs, anemones, starfish and all the local shellfish were to be found behind curtains of seaweed. In the tidal puddles, tiny flat fish hid in the sand and hermit crabs scurried about carrying their little dwellings, while treasures such as the iridescent oyster valves and egg-cases of deep-water fish were to be found along with the sand tracks of our earlier dawn chorus. But the *punt* added another dimension to our explorations around the bay and the *sgeirans*, which we were able to board to the shrieks of nesting gulls and terns, as seals and cormorants took to the water. Off the precipitous southern end of the island the waters run dark and deep and the great round head of a massive rock can just be seen in the depths at low tide, with tendrils of seaweed like the curled tresses of a monster wavering about with the tidal drift. But there were real monsters out there – the basking sharks or 'sail-fish', so called for their large dorsal fins, when fleets of them arrived just off shore. Seeing such a 30-foot monster breach – burst clear out of the sea – was spectacular, and when it did so but a few yards from the *punt*, creating its own *tsunami*, one's heart beat just a little faster and we pulled up our lines till the commotion passed.

We swam inside the old fish trap loop over sand which gave warmth to the tide and, outwith the regularity of eating and sleeping, the only partition of the day was the arrival and departure of the MacBrayne steamer on its daily visit to the village a mile away to the south, where naval craft popped in and out and the puffer, making more smoke than the steamer, arrived from time to time with its load of coal.

Peace

But these pre-pubescent years were coming to a close along with the Second World War, to be superseded by a tough adolescence and the conscious matter of growing up. We built the victory bonfires of old herring boxes up on the castle 'Land' and soon after that I accompanied Alistair MacFarlane, my father's 'best man' cousin from Glasgow, to the village on his return from five years in a *stalag* in Poland, having been torpedoed in the first month of the war and not having seen his second son Roy until we arrived by bus at the quay, hung with bunting and 'Welcome Home Alistair'. This was how I saw the end of the war that had governed so much of our young lives, within the strange parameters of a temporary matriarchy of feisty women, two grandmothers who ruled their respective roosts and an intelligent extrovert mother whose eclectic enthusiasms portrayed something of a romantic sensibility, which I am told has rubbed off on me; and, from a look at my own enthusiasms, I would have to agree that there may be some truth in that.

But the celebratory hiatus of victory was short-lived: and it is with some reluctance that I think of the miserable greyness that followed the war years, with an exhausted adult population low in spirit and resources depleted from that great struggle to end the Nazi rampage. Within this general air of depression, the condition of our domestic scene was exacerbated by my mother's benevolent open-door policy and my father's easy complacency on such matters, giving rise to an uncomfortable lack of space and privacy, with nowhere but the garden shed in which to hide.

With father's demob a new little sister Christine, part of the country's baby boom, arrived; and this marked the end of his life afloat, begun in 1916 during the First World War when he left school at 14 to join his father at the herring fishing before going 'deep sea' in 1922. Now he returned to a nine-to-five white-collar clerical job, and it has always appeared to me that he did so to please my mother. There could have been little positive in this change for someone whose skills and craft had been gleaned from a life at sea; and photographs of this time provide an image that confirms my memory of him as less than happy with his altered circumstances. It is not difficult to appreciate the problem of coming to terms with such 'normality', for one who had sailed the waters of the western Arctic, been shipwrecked in the ice of Ungava Bay, and serviced Pitcairn Island annually throughout the 1930s on passages to Australia, before surviving a lively and dangerous Second World War in the Atlantic. The bond of the sea that was obvious to me in the fellowship of seafaring shared between the familial males of that generation was inimitable, on a quite

The Bayeskimo, *Hudson Bay supply ship, became locked and lost in the ice of Ungava Bay, on my father's first trip to the Arctic in 1925.*

The Nascopie, *with reinforced steel bow, that picked the crew of the* Bayeskimo *up from the ice in 1925 and on which my father crewed in 1928.*

My father, in sea-boots, on the Baychimo *in 1927. She also was lost in the ice, in 1931, but freed herself and floated about for some years, to be known as the 'Ghost Ship' of the Arctic, last sighted in 1956.*

different scale to the recreational pleasure of messing about in boats, as Conrad put it : 'one is only the amusement of life and the other is life itself'.

His firmness in dealing with me was neither more nor less than the normal father/son relationship of these days: much of it I believe related to his view that I had been born with a silver spoon in my mouth. There was some truth in that, coming as it did from someone who thought himself lucky getting an orange for a childhood Christmas. He was yet only 47 and it would be some 20 years before he was settled again in his native village, taking up once more the friendships of his early years and many of the ploys concerning boats and the hunting of fish and fowl for the pot.

Happy days – and I would regularly find myself joining some ancients heading out of the harbour at dusk to try our luck at the 'plash' – a traditional method of catching salmon (always known as the 'queer fellow') at locations where fresh water entered the sea loch. They were very good at it and rarely returned empty-handed, but even more impressive was their uncanny knowledge of where they were, in the pitch black of early morning when a thick sea mist might arrive and one could only see the lit ends of their cigarettes as they sat in the stern, yarning happily about times gone by – my father, Snessie, and Robert MacFarlane, Rufus, at 12 years old, with one of their jackets, a valuable garment in 1914, left on the shore of Skate Island where they had been shooting duck and dookers, and they laugh as they reminisce on rowing all the way back to collect it with blistered hands, in a *punt* full of sea birds as provisioning for their families. Here in the mist I wondered at their navigational skills as we confidently covered the nautical miles, until out of the mist popped the red light of the perch as we entered the harbour. It still surprises me – that ancient sensory skill that is acutely linked to assessments of space and time; and one might say that they knew much more than they were able or interested in telling. Seascape geography informed their senses, as did their repositories of ancient and real-time history that were as important to them as their daily victuals.

Although that generation did not look it, in the photographs of them dressed in navy-blue serge in their 1930s prime, they were not too far removed from an earlier world of barter economics and hunter-gatherers. They may even have taken offence at such a suggestion, but my father's brother Finlay told how in 1913 the princely sum of £5 was the only money earned when the herring fishing failed, and my father told of my grandfather's uncharacteristically brutal reaction to Finlay, at the age of 13 in that year, falling on the ice of Laggan Loch and breaking the stock of the gun, the weapon that brought black cock and hare to the table. The vitals were provided by the gun, line fishing and stored grain, along with the collection of wild fruit and nuts in season, pillow slips filled with hazelnuts collected on Baravala being but one example of the natural world providing some relief in these hard times.

But, in lives so influenced by the sea, there was little sense of grievance in their reminiscences of hardship, which was quite at variance from the well-recorded tyranny imposed on those whose lives were dictated by the daily grind of making a living from the land.

There was common sense tempered by droll humour to almost all of their experience, including that of severe hardship, and to those that carried a sense of action there would often be the descriptive 'ploy' that certainly covered all poaching activities. To the outsider's heavy usage of 'beautiful' when talking of Argyll and thereabouts, the local worthy might respond, 'But you canna eat it', although I suspect that he would have been at ease with Henri Poincaré's 'care for the beautiful leads us to the same selection as care for the useful'. They were acutely aware of the aesthetics that were linked to the crafts in which they, as non-specialists, excelled, and could turn their hands to a great assortment of tasks in materials as different as wood, metal and rope. I think particularly of Matt McDougall, a lobster fisherman, whose boat was constructed from the hull of a Portuguese liner's carvel-built life-boat, exquisitely remodelled to the needs of the solitary creeler. Along with my father, he visited me to share a dram when I had completed the reconstruction of an old attic space apartment for our family and, while complimenting me on the quality of the new accommodation, he said of the stair handrail that he held in his hand, 'Erchie, you might think to take an arris turn on this as it's a wheen on the sharp side' – this hand was rock-like after being inured to some 70 years of salt sea, yet where did he find the 'arris'?

Expression could be quite lyrical on occasion and not uncommonly ran in families. Some 30 years earlier, his nephew Willie (Tar) McDougall suggested that we take a little trip with his daughter Wilma and my daughter Kathryn on a fine Sunday morning. He had a *punt* with outboard engine lying at the West Loch Tarbert pier and off we set down the loch past Eilean da Ghallagain and the settlements of Torinturk and Achnaglach on the north shore. The girls were five years old and, while we chatted about the natural life around us, Willie asked Wilma to make the call of a wigeon, which she did; with accomplished sharp variable whistles of the male and quiet little growls of the female of the species. This was followed by a variety of seabird calls to which she had been introduced by her father. It came as no surprise that this little girl moved on to a successful career in opera some years later.

Schooling 1947

But back in the city in 1947, I left the little primary school that had provided such a pleasant jaunt and my city orientation moved south across the River Clyde as a pupil for the following six years at Hutchesons Grammar School, founded in 1650, around which Glasgow's most notorious district, the Gorbals, had developed; housing successive waves of immigrants, particularly from famine in Ireland and Jewish pogroms in the part of Russia that had previously been in the Polish–Lithuanian Commonwealth. It probably had the feel of New York's Bronx, and there were stories, not necessarily apocryphal, of new arrivals thinking that was where they were!

The move to the new school saw the loosening of strings from the nest, given impetus by the physical distance between the two. By the time I left school in1953 they were hanging by a thread. But for these six years I cycled to school from the city's northern boundary after a daily milk-round that saw a very early rise, which to this day has me in accord with Spinoza's view of the luxury of a 'long lie', that may nurture our more interesting speculations. Nor did such exertions provide a solution to my rugby coach's annual directive to put more flesh on my skinny but wiry adolescent frame. Little did he know of the daily morning labour in all sorts of weather that would have been thought of as character-building by my parents and others, but as little short of barbaric now.

It was shared with half-a-dozen other guys from the white-collar, blue-collar and no-collar mix of the local social background. We dived about like wraiths in the icy pre-dawn gloom, shifting enormous quantities of glass-bottled milk in steel carriers to mainly tenement housing from a moving van driven by an ex-soldier task-master, where all was done at the run. For this I was paid 15 shillings a week that more than covered the outlay for a 'fancy' school while the hardship proved instructive in an altogether different context, namely 'girls'. By my mid-teen years it was noticeable that the guys of the 'no-collar' lot were light-years more street-wise about the opposite sex than were we, who were making such connections up in our heads, as the girls with whom we mixed had no intention of helping us out. So, in the little spare time that we had, a couple of us took to pastures new and connections with girls from other districts who could help us along. When I hear Sheena Wellington's anthem 'Strong Women', I am pleased to recall the mill girls of Paisley, rather than of Sheena's feisty Dundee.

The schooling that straddled the terrain of adolescence was, in comparison to the earlier years, equally tough. Gone was the soft, encouraging touch of the female teachers, replaced by an altogether harsher male regime. The teaching staff was, to a man – and they were all male but for a solitary French teacher – a dour bunch who stuck to their mandates of bland instruction in their particular specialisations that was helped along with the regular threat and use of the tawse. They were just ordinary Joes whose teaching careers had in most cases been interrupted by a war that was less than an enlightening experience, and we youngsters were at the receiving end of their frustrations and the normal authoritarian attitudes of the time. One might have expected an individual teacher to have demonstrated an alternative milder learning option, but it was not to be. We accepted it as the norm and got on with it, but some years later, in the Edinburgh of 1957, the works of the inspirational teacher A S Neill came my way, recording many of these ills and promoting another way. The obituary in *The Times* on his death in 1973, 'If children are happier nowadays than their elders sometimes it is due in no small measure to this craggy, lovable Scot', is a modest appreciation of the man, while his own preface to *Dominie's Log*, 'As a boy I attended a village school where the bairns chattered and were happy. I trace my love of freedom to my free life there, and I dedicate this book to my former dominie, my father,' suggests the value of a more relaxed option.

It is indeed ironic that this Scotland, which in its 18th-century Enlightenment had floated the ideas of the 'Democratic Intellect' and the significance of generalist education to the world, should have burdened its children with an authoritarian educational form to feed its specialist professions. I could not make these connections at the time, when I was more interested in chasing girls or a ball, but before I was much older the more obvious shortfalls of this education were apparent. The lack of exposure to the inter-relationships of the individual subjects of our studies, where simple connections between mathematics and the arts might well have encouraged our interest. Even now, when such proposals are presented to educational authorities and the good sense of such linkages is agreed, the problem of already-crammed curricula arises.

Although the study of maths still appears to be less than attractive to many students, the abstract manner of the teaching method surely contributes to the difficulty. By the age of ten we have all experienced rhythm in music and dance, and an introduction to maths through such exemplars could provide a basis for its understanding. Linkages to the order in nature are exposed in the simple mathematics of Fibonacci's numerical sequences, occurring dramatically in the compound spirals of the shells on the beach and the sunflower's head, the helical patterns of growth that exist within nature's profusion, and budding Clark Maxwells and D'Arcy Thompsons would surely be taken by that seductive magic.

If the scholastic tedium was bleak, the school building itself was as black as the colourless world of the industrial city outwith its walls. An open grate fire in every classroom provided meagre heat and it says something when the scent of burnt orange peel provides a solitary pleasant memory of the place. Solid schoolboy friendships were to provide a redeeming factor along with the game of rugby, to which I was a convert at the age of twelve. The game with the oval ball also provided my first introduction to Edinburgh, where our international rugby matches were played, and it was during such a weekend that cousins of my mother from the Isle of Skye revealed to my young eyes the amazing urban core of this other city, but 42 miles from Glasgow – a visit that was later to provide a locale as important to me as that of the fishing village.

Ring-Net Fishing

If schooling was now a chore, the pattern of life – school year in the city and summers in the village – continued, and memory is packed with the intensity of the latter, where the longstanding family history in Tarbert allowed access to much of the culture-mass, relating to land and sea, that I have attempted to imbue in my own offspring – something of a 'dooker' inheritance.

The 1930s had witnessed one of the recurring cycles when herring deserted Loch Fyne, but the war's end saw their reappearance in abundance, coinciding with the availability of government grants for the purchase of new fishing boats that were taken up by returning servicemen. A new fleet of ring-netters was created and boom time arrived in Tarbert with the

Aerial photograph of part of Tarbert harbour, with some 60 ring-netters on their moorings. (Photographer unknown)

The quay, early evening in 1948, with ring-netters about to leave for a night's fishing. Two of my pals sit in the bow of the Mary Bain, *while I take the photograph with a Box Brownie.*

quay as the hub to the associated boatyards, sail-lofts, barking sheds and smokehouses. It was not the tidiest of villages and acquired a pungent odour from the mountains of fish boxes on the quay and the low-tide wrack, which some found offensive. My grandmother had two nieces, the genteel daughters of her sister Kate and a wealthy southerner, who would arrive by steamer. They held pomaded silk to their refined nebs as they passed the quay and would plant great red kisses on me, if found, much to my consternation and the glee of my pals. However, there was an occasion when my own olfactory sense was sorely tried and I would have been pleased to have had the pomaded silk – a large Minke whale had been beached, on the shore below Dougie Leitch's shed, just inside the perch light, and a timber scaffold erected around it, from which two worthies with a two-handed saw cut great slices of blubber. The smell was gargantuan and seemed to become lodged deep within one's being, as no matter how often one blew one's nose it would not clear – thus was whaling excluded from my early seafaring career ambitions. Although some years were to pass before they were finally extinguished, when my father decided that I was going nowhere on a ship, after he decoded a message from the seaman's pool in Glasgow inviting me for a medical, for which I had signed up in an attempted escape from secondary schooling.

But over and above the occasional whale, and amidst all the hustle and bustle of village life, there were little pockets of sophistication among my grandmother's friends, for whom I did small services – Katy Allan's Pier House, where the walls were lined with panels of butterflies of iridescent azure blue which the National Museum might envy, and then Flora and Marion Murray's flat with south-facing orange and red stained glass, setting the varnished timber floor and its oriental rugs aflame. But the ring-net boats with their sleek lines were the stars in my affection. They were slender, sharp-prowed vessels with substance in their ample canoe sterns, and they sparkled in bright varnish, their normal finish in the early post-war years. They lay three- four- and five-deep along the quay at weekends, dressed in the ordered attire of carefully shipped nets and ancillary lines, poles and baskets; quite extraordinary the care and finesse with which boats and gear were left, that had but hours earlier been battered by the nature of their labour and the fickle weather of the fishing grounds.

Angus Martin wrote: 'Few boys growing up in a fishing village can resist the spell of boats and fishermen. There is a mystery in the movement of a fleet at evening. Men go out into the night with a purpose. If the purpose is fulfilled, they return in the morning with fish; if it isn't fulfilled, they return anyway and seem no different. The mystery lies out at sea, in the darkness. In sea-time, the familiar, comforting land becomes a

THE QUAY
TARBERT

disjointed memory, a dream almost. Herring fishermen work in the night, when most people are at home, secure in bed. What happens out there when men hunt and kill herring?' Thinking that my father might help in satisfying my curiosity, I asked how I should go about getting aboard a 'ringer'. He advised that I wander along the quay of an evening, when the crews sat about on deck yarning and smoking and I should make a choice. This was not quite what I was looking for, thinking that it would be a simple matter for him to ask one of his relatives or friends on my behalf, but no – you were expected to get on with things yourself in this world. It was an awesome task at the age of eleven to consider approaching any of these tough, weather-beaten ancients, but, summoning up courage, I did as advised, curiously choosing Archie MacCaig of the *Seonaid*, whose boat was one of the oldest in the fleet with probably the oldest crew. With them I went on to spend my boyhood summers in a truly life-enhancing ploy. It occurs to me that I must have been serious about it, as I gave up the free summer evenings of those testosterone-fuelled years and the manic adolescent interest in those of the opposite sex.

The choice had to have been one of simple chance, as I only knew the skipper and crew from seeing them on the quay, although some were, like many of the fishermen, 'forty-second cousins' – but whatever my reasoning, it was a fortunate one. Major technical advances were coming into the fleet and soon every boat would have 'walkie-talkie', allowing two-way transmission between boats, and the 'echo-sounder', providing images of the seabed and fish life in between; but not the *Seonaid* or her neighbour the *Sweet Marie*, who would continue to hunt herring entirely by the traditional sensory methods of sight, sound, smell and touch.

This was indeed an education and one that would have been lost to me if I had come along ten or so years later. There were numerous 'signs' in the search for herring shoals – the regular presence of that 'imperial fish hunter', the solan (gannet), the height of its strike telling something of the depth and the species of its prey; the significance of the presence of the whale, nibbling its way around the perimeter of a shoal; but more dramatically, our looking for signs of the shoal in the phosphorescence (*the burning*) while lying forward in the bow with an experienced crewman and striking the gunwale's steel plate with the anchor shank, causing the shoal to start and producing an incandescent flash in the plankton's phosphorescent glow. Or, on a quiet night at dusk, listening intently for the very specific clean 'plout' of a herring that distinguished it from mackerel, lythe (pollock) and other species; while, on the move, the weighted wire trailed over the stern could register the impact of striking fish at particular

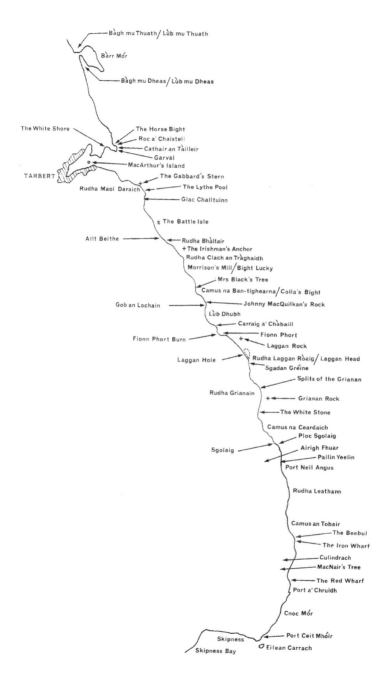

Map of fishermen's place-names along the Tarbert West Shore. (Angus Martin)

depths, the vibration telling the experienced fisherman the density of the shoal.

The ring-net fleet, and it could amount to 80 boats, left the harbour in pairs in the early summer evening, the departure time dependent on our particular destination. But if we were to stay in Loch Fyne, then we might go across and lie at anchor alongside our neighbour-boat in Buck's Bay, where over mugs of tea and slices of toast the skippers and crew would discuss likely tactics for the night. The location reminds me of an occasion when I was all of thirteen and the task of provisioning the boat for the week had been delegated to me by Archie 'Ja' MacDougall, whose responsibility it was. So on a bright Monday morning in August I set off to the quay-side chandlers with a trolley and cash, and having filled it with plain loaves, tea, sugar, tinned milk, etc, I discovered that there was about £1 to spare. Having been told to use all the cash, I looked around the shelves and decided on the purchase of a box of Christmas puddings. That evening, awaiting dusk in Buck's Bay, I prepared the first bite of the night. The pudding cans were brought out of the locker and the instructions carefully read: 'Simmer for five minutes and cover can as you open'. As the skipper was at the tiller, puffing on a pipe, I took his mug of tea, toast and Christmas pudding aft to him. He took one look at the offering and asked what it might be. 'A Christmas pudding, Mr MacCaig', I explained. After a momentary silence, MacCaig let out a roar: 'But this is the fucking month of August!' I got below as quickly as possible, to the amusement of the ancient crew, who had foreseen the likely reaction when they saw me, bull-headed opener and can in hand. Archie 'Ja' later told me that the outcome of this venture was that when there was a good 'fishing' and any extra pennies, the *Seonaid* sailed with Christmas puddings from that day on; thus my sole contribution to the affairs of herring fishing on Loch Fyne.

If, however, we were off south to the Kilbrannan Sound, I would be sitting on the fish hold boards with 'Dorby' (Malcolm MacFarlane), who, when not showing me tricks that he could perform with a Woodbine cigarette, would have me repeat the names of the coastal fishing marks between Tarbert and Skipness on the outward trip and have me confirm their retention in my young head the following morning as we headed home along that West Shore, to which Dorby would often add his two-pence worth – the Battle Isle (*Eilean a'chomhraig*) – 'Dirty grun in there an fill o' widow's laces' (rough boulder seabed with cover of *Chorda filum* up to 15 metres long) – or, to get me really interested, as we passed the deep seabed trench off Lagan, where herring could lurk at daybreak – 'Wonder if that fella's in his bathysphere doon there the day' as the Royal Navy was carrying out some tests with such equipment from the village at that time. The Battle Isle could have more singular importance than Dorby's description, as the location of a *Bellum Maritimum*, the first sea battle recorded in the history of the British Isles, is thought to have taken place close to Tarbert, a stronghold of the victors, the *Cenel nGabrainn*. Had I been able to tell him of this event, he would after a moment or two, have brought my dreaming to earth with something like: 'Well, that crew wid need more nor a bowl o' porridge for sic a ploy' (those involved in such a battle would require a hearty breakfast).

The spoken language on the skiff was still sprinkled with the last of the living Gaelic from these parts and the mnemonic device of a culture, the place-names, carried the cognitive story map of the coast. It was intricate and four-dimensional, as the language variation of Gaelic, Norse, Scots and English illustrates. But now, 70 years distance from Dorby and the West Shore, who needs a cognitive map in their brain when every phone provides a Google map? But sadly the less we need to develop cognitive maps of our own, the less understanding are we likely to have of all the byways and seaways.

But back with the *Seonaid* and the night dark came exciting times – the boats worked in pairs and one had to be aware of the neighbour's location especially on a dark loch busy with boats. When the neighbour *shot* (fed out its net) we were required to pick up the *winky* (lit net end) and both boats would then tow the great loop of the net to close as a ring. The *shot* saw great activity, and for this boy all the drama and immediacy of *Dive, Dive, Dive!* in the submariner movies of the war, as the *winky* was sought out and taken aboard. The adrenalin rush continued as the crew of the boat which had made the *shot* was now joined by the crew of the neighbour, boarding in the dark in sea-boots and oilskins on a pitching deck to assist with the haul, while the neighbour now held the hauling boat off the net. The haul began and then the first signs of herring in the meshes and some *craic* (chat) on the likely outcome of the *shot*, followed by the taking aboard of the catch by the stick baskets or later by *brailer* (narrow meshed net bag used to scoop herring from the net to the boat). The boats split off, the net was *redd* (clearing debris) and returned to the port quarter and the hunt began again. There may have been two or three *shots* before dawn appeared and the herring disappeared and we would turn back to the village. I would see to the fish kettle going onto the stove with a load of herring, boiled in brine and served around with toast from the fo'c's'le stove, below if the weather was unkind or up on deck when it was fine. Most evocative of that time of day is George Campbell Hay's poem:

The Kerry Shore

Blow, good wind from westward, blow against the dawn,
blow across this livid loch with shadows strawn.
Sweetly blew the breeze from westward, o'er she lay,
Coming down the Kerry Shore at break of day.

Up from hills of dreaming Cowal came the sun,
clear he stood and struck with fire the waters dun,
waves green-sided, bright, white-crested glittered gay,
coming down the Kerry Shore at break of day.

Head on Tarbert, through the seas she raised a cry,
jewels of foam around her shoulders tossed on high,
green waves rose about her bows and broke away,
coming down the Kerry Shore at break of day.

And to be greeted, as we entered the outer harbour and passed the perch light, with the smell of fresh baking, the prevailing early morning odour carried on light westerlies from the village bakers. I would go ashore for the morning rolls while the sample basket of herring went into the market. If we were early we might see the laborious task of discharging the catch, by winched basket from the hold to boxes on lorries on the quay, completed by early morning, when the *Seonaid* would be taken over to her daily rest alongside the *Sweet Marie* at their mooring just west of Dickie's Yard, until the following evening's foray.

Then home to the old Argyll House and a slunge down before going to my gran's front bedroom to stoke the smouldering fire before heading for 'blanket bay' myself. This village adolescence, like childhood, seems to have had a surfeit of sunshine and my memory of awakening was to the light lace window curtains floating in the afternoon's warm summer breeze with the brightly lit harbour beyond. On one occasion I was brought quickly into the waking world when I heard old Ned McCallien, the shoemaker on the ground floor, blethering on the street to the local bobby who was telling him that he was going to warm young *Snessie*'s behind (our family nickname from the Gaelic *sneachd* for snow for our fair hair) for practising long jumps over wooden fish boxes and throwing the thirteenth, which he invariably went through, into the harbour. I was probably in training for the 1948 Olympics at the time but, in any case, gave the bobby a wide berth for the rest of the summer.

The boys of the village tended to grow up with more of an interest in the sea or the hill, depending on which part of the village they lived in, and in these summer months mine could be located as between low- and high-water mark. Although I might be found around stook-building in the hay time of late summer at the head of the West Loch or around any of the adults when out with the gun, most of the endless summer hours were spent in *punts* around the shore. The basic skills of rowing and sculling were well-honed, as were the sea-knots and the handling of fishing-lines.

What great good fortune it was that this place had a poet of the quality of George Campbell Hay, to leave to us a lyrical record of both the sea and the hill.

Poetry in my early youth meant song – the Gaelic, or the Scots of Robert Burns – but the school's introductions to such classics as Milton's *Paradise Lost*, of which I could not hold ten lines in my head, did no favours to any budding interest in the muse, in much the same way as the church's message of Original Sin saw to an early dismissal of what religion had on offer.

GCH's first collected works, *Wind on Loch Fyne,* came my way shortly after its publication in 1956, and my stride on Edinburgh's cobbles caught the rhythm of the lyric poetry that gave measure and body to my early experience of the same coasts and the fishings on that great herring loch.

I think of his poems 'Laggan' and 'Laggan Roaig', where three burns rush from the upper moorland to converge in a tight ragged gorge, all but smothered in green, before spreading through the white boulder shore of Fionnaport to the sea. Hay sets it in a 'smoky smirr o' rain' just enlivened by 'a wee wae cheep' of a woodland bird, and the set is utterly convincing. He does it time and again in landward themes and, from experience he gained aboard Calum Johnson's skiff, the *Liberator*, he produces its equal in wonderful pacy verse at sea.

The *Liberator* was partnered in the years before the Second World War by the *Seonaid*, which, in the years following the war, was partner of the *Sweet Marie,* skippered by a Smith cousin of my grandmother, and grandfather of the late John Smith, leader of the UK Labour Party. This was all quite coincidental to my summers on the *Seonaid*, but, when Hay died in 1984, I thought that his memory might be promoted by the illustration of some of his work and particularly through his great sea poem 'Seeker, Reaper' – but more of that venture later…

The Gaelic Shadow

Throughout the Glasgow school days I would take advantage of short holidays and cycle to the old fish market where I would get a lift by fish lorry, my bike roped on top of empty boxes, and head west for Tarbert. It must have been on one such autumnal trip that the 'Badger's Moon' (The moon that catches winter) entered my head. It is the moon that follows that of harvest and is described in the Gaelic as *Gealach Buidhe nam Broc*, and it was around this time that I began to grasp the scale of loss of the language that could so easily have been part of my early make-up. I was not the first to notice it. The wife of Sir Donald MacAlister of Tarbert records that 'It was the consciousness of the loss which he had himself sustained that led Sir Donald, when President of An Comunn Gaidhealach, to emphasise in his Presidential Address in 1908, the folly of neglecting Gaelic and the importance of enabling Highland children to keep their priceless heritage of being bi-lingual'.

Every nook and cranny of Highland Scotland appears to have a name, and the Ordnance Survey was somewhat kinder in the recording of them than was the case just across the North Channel in Ireland. Although the spoken language has gone from most of the land, the Gaelic-named landscape is still with us and walking the land without it puts one, in my reckoning, at a scale of disadvantage as that of a one-legged man. Although I have some useful vocabulary I am regularly stumped as to the meanings and stories of place. As an instance of which, I had for years visited by sea a little landing place sheltered by *sgeirans* just south of Barmore. It was called Port a'chuill and I thought that 'chuil', a reference to coal, had to be a cartographer's mistake. I mentioned it to a Tarbert forester friend who confirmed that it was indeed a reference to coal… indeed charcoal, as it had been worked nearby. The detailed description of charcoal-burning on Barmore had been discovered quite by chance and written up by John Fowlis in his *Landscapes and Lives*.

Something of what can be appreciated of the past has been helped along by familiarity not only with Loch Fyne but also with the Atlantic shores of Kintyre and Knapdale, their raised beaches, sea lochs and coves of sand and rock and particularly of a favoured one, that I come across by chance from the sea on a lobster-fishing summer in 1955.

Named Loch Stornoway, with the same meaning from the Norse (Steering Bay) as its larger namesake in Lewis, it is a wide sandy bay facing west. A burn runs from the pocket of rough hill country that bounds it, in a meander to the sea through a flood plain and the bay's sandy shore. Three standing stones, that may form an alignment with the Spring Equinox, and a little burial ground mark historic time. They tell of settlement that pre-dates the nearby ferry-point of Ardpatrick and the coming of the Scotti. The life of intervening centuries is caught in the mute rubble of croft ruins, sitting just above the white sand shore through which a trickle runs, rippled red from an iron oxide spring; while the ancient language rings in the voices of the children who would have danced around that shore, among the now wizened remnants of a kitchen garden's apple and cherry tree.

The heady scent of bog myrtle prevails, as it does on much of the coast, and would that it could be bottled. We dug some up and it was successfully rooted in a pot by my city bedroom door, where I am reminded of the west with every touch of its leaf. Some years ago, after an evening meal in a Sardinian coastal village, we were invited by the waitress to try a liquor of the country which turned out to be Myrto, distilled from a relative of our Bog Myrtle (Sweet Gale), that covered every stony hillside, and although it didn't carry the weight of fragrance as that from our Atlantic shore, the flavour from the bottle carried the scent.

For centuries the settlement at Loch Stornoway was known as Lergnahension, 'the slope of the ash', a quiet reminder of the Gaelic language taking the names of the 18 letters of its alphabet from trees. But that name, like so many others, has vanished from the maps and is now more commonly known as Carse (extensive alluvial land along the banks of a river). A rich tapestry of names jumps from the early maps. At the northern headland of the bay, one may take one's pick from the imagery suggested by the name Rudha Cruitiridh (the point of the hunchback or the harpist) while others relate to lingering folk tales of witchcraft and magical events that were connected to a celebrated clan battle. On the hill just behind the headland there is a rock ledge Creag a' Stars onto which if you are able to flick a pebble, as many still do, you will have your heart's desire. It was from this rock that the *cailleach* (old woman) horse goddess reputedly disappeared skyward, deserting the field of battle, while no horse will pass along, but with reluctance, the haunted roadside hollow below.

It is a quite magical pickle and one can get caught up in the spirit of it when the uncanny occurs. While scraping mussels for a shell-fish brew on the shore, from exposed rocks that lay between the tides, a polished stone tool made for that purpose in Neolithic times appeared at our feet (in the photograph) from some loose sand and grit among the actual rocks! Its rounded form echoes the hollow of the user's cupped hand

and a tool has never been made that better fits, while the same may be said of its purpose, scraper at one end and little hammer at the other. I was demonstrating in my hand and that of my eight-year-old grandson how it might have been used, and when casually suggesting that it was a most treasured possession he said nothing but looked at me askance in

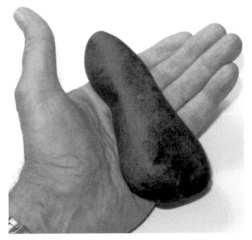

The Stone Scraper.

a house full of the appurtenances of modern life. He will learn.

An earlier occasion, magical but hardly uncanny, found me listening to my son Ruaridh of 12 years explaining that the latest carbon-fibre Japanese fishing rod was an essential tool. It was a fine day and I had him accompany me to a small cane plantation on the Stonefield estate from which I cut a substantial cane and back in the village I took from my shed an eight inch steel brad and some wire. We sat outside the kitchen door and with hammer and file flattened and fashioned a hook at one end of the brad and slotted and wired the other end into a housing split in the cane. Off we went to the Lergnahension burn and to still water at mid-tide. We waded in, he to his oxters and myself to the waist, and very slowly and carefully looked for the two black dots in the sand that might give away the plaice or the flounder's location. As luck would have it, the dots appeared and the spear did its deadly best, with a plaice that was large enough to cut into steaks. I have to admit to being as surprised as my son at its size but it put paid to further reference to Japanese fishing rods for at least two weeks.

The Lergnahension Burn at low water and Ruaridh, still in the burn with the spear that had brought success earlier in the day. The island of Gigha lies off, in the distance.

I think of Loch Stornoway and its headlands as open world territory, with the islands of the southern Hebrides, Islay, Jura and Gigha lying offshore and the Atlantic stretching to infinity beyond. But the coastal land that runs back from it along the shores of West Loch Tarbert provides an altogether different, more intimate and private world. For much of its seven miles it is a wildwood that we know to replicate the natural temperate rainforest that has for millennia thrived on the acidic soils of western Scotland. Small oak joins the birch, hazel and holly that grow with the sloe, the 'gean' (cherry) and the honeysuckle in some profusion and where every boulder and much of the arboreal bark is covered in lichen.

It has a dream quality, lit softly through its deciduous canopy, while the scents of the complex undergrowth pervade the senses and I could fancy that W B Yeats had such a locale in mind when he wrote 'The Song of Wandering Aengus'. Not so far-fetched as the tapestry of names that so enlivens the precincts of Loch Stornoway here in this woodland carries cultural links to the arrival of the Scots from Ireland some 1500 years ago.

There are seven Iron Age forts on the West Loch, from the impressive vitrified Dun Skeig that guards its entrance from the Atlantic to the relatively well-preserved Dun a Choin Dhuibh. They are the theatrical props to the story of the surrounding landscape – the ill-fated love of Diarmuid and Grianne and the epic boar hunt of Diarmuid and the warrior host of the Fianna around Sliabh Ghaoil (the Mount of Love). High drama is never far removed from the mythology and just as we have the flying horse goddess above Loch Stornoway, here we have the boar in flight from the hunters as it lands across the Loch at Leamnamuic (the pig's leap). I move the corrugated sheet that covers the roadside well (Tobar Aonghais) for a sip of its clear spring water whenever I pass and tip my hat to this fellow who had the hermit priest's cell nearby that gave name to the adjacent lochan (Loch Cill an Aonghais). Perhaps he preached to the Fianna who were surely the wild west show of these far off days!

In a clearing of the woodland nearby there was a cottage belonging to my mother's friend, Kirsty, who also came from the Isle of Skye. On the occasion of my first visit on an autumnal day, she proffered a refreshment from a substantial pot that sat warming by an open peat fire. It was my introduction to sloe gin and I have never tasted another like it. The Gaelic conversation of the two old ladies was most appropriate in this congenial setting and a sparkle was added to it, not only by the sloe gin, but by the acoustic reverberation that danced along off a multitude of enamel and china teapots that crammed every wall space. I collected sloes from that patch for many years thereafter but my beverage never achieved the light quality of dear Kirsty's.

The local historian Marion Campbell's 'All around us the past has fed the present' comes to mind. This is not the Wild Scotland so eagerly being sought by backpackers. It is territory defined by geography of land and sea that is in itself delightful but enriched by the cultural wealth of reference recording human interaction, whether in the naming of its storied landscape or artefacts and blocks of stone.

A prediction of the end of the herring fishing came to me from my father's old friend Matt MacDougall. In his garden above the village he was giving me a lobster, packed in a shoe box with wood shavings, to take back for an evening meal in the city, and looking down on the quiet Sunday harbour he said 'There willna be a pair o' ringers oot o' here in ten years' time', and so it came to pass. Matt himself did not last long after this but went out with what I would consider proper Tarbert elan. I went into a crowded Tarbert Hotel of a weekend evening, where Matt was holding court at the bar: 'I'm just telling them, Erchie, that these are the steps o' "Ladies o' Spain I Adore Thee"', and looked for my approval of some intricate footwork. I, of course, was willing to please and after some further nonsense I saw him off at the door. It was the last any of us saw of this fine old character in life, as he was found the following morning sitting peacefully in his armchair in front of a lifeless fire.

His going brought an end to the snug den that was his shed, lying on the north shore of the inner harbour and redolent of the seafaring life. It smelt of everything that defined the place, the pungent odour of ropes and nets that had seen much of the barking yard's protection, the pot-bellied iron stove doing its bit with exotic hardwood off-cuts from the nearby boatyard, along with lighter and fresher wafts of sea wrack from the

Matt's Shed & his lobster boat, the Rose (Crayon & Pencil sketches).

harbour waters outside the open door. The tea kettle sat permanently on the stove, its black stewed offering improved by not just a drop of canned condensed milk but the drop of whisky from the bottle hidden in the blanket of nets hanging over the roof's open joists. It was a place for yarns, to which Matt's fine creel boat swinging on its mooring just beyond the door gave substance.

My father predeceased him in 1984 by a couple of years and it marked something of the manner in which the village still treated a bereavement, of which I knew nothing. He went quite rapidly from being frail to infirm and passed away quietly in his own home. I was in Edinburgh but my wife Dorothy was with my mother and she contacted Agatha, a retired village nurse, when he died in the early hours of the morning and she came immediately. She was an old friend of my father and had been born at Baravalla, where he had collected the autumnal hazelnut crop as a boy. My mother sat tearfully by the fire, and Agatha explained to Dorothy that 'things will have to be done by you and me, rather than strangers'. Dorothy's background was that of a city girl and she was quite taken aback, but went with the nurse and together they stripped, bathed and prepared the body for the arrival of the doctor and his confirmation of the cause of death. She had been very fond of him and has since expressed how important this final service was to her, although a shock to her system at the time.

It was probably the end of the tradition of the womenfolk taking care of such matters, while traditionally the carpenter from Dickie's boatyard would have made a simple wooden coffin. In recent times the same fellow would come into the front bar of the Tarbert Hotel on a Friday evening, standing at the end away from the traditional fishing fraternity, one of whom might say 'Keep yir eyes off o' me, Mac…'

Agatha was a stalwart, just one of that generation of women who ruled domestic life during times of world war and less than easy peace, but, like their menfolk, they could find humour in almost every experience. Dorothy and my mother would visit Flora MacAlpine, a dear friend of my mother's, and from her repertoire of stories she told how, as a little girl, she and two siblings with measles were placed in a darkened room, to protect their sight, in the large family bed. Their mother placed a paper poke (bag) over each of their heads with a hole for feeding purposes, and Flora said, 'If you didnae gae blind wi' the measles ye'd gae deif wi' the rustlin' o' the paper pokes'. Thus were life's trials diminished.

Profession

Before school days ended in 1953 I had to consider future employment options. If I was not going to sea then the school subjects of interest, the Maths, Art, English and History, would work well with the choice of architecture, which was supported by the art teacher and, probably more significantly, by my English teacher, who thought that I had some fluency in describing buildings and places. To the family it was a strange choice and greeted with incomprehension, as there was not even a brickie in our tribe let alone an architect, nor would anyone have been able to put a name to such a fellow.

A professional apprenticeship offered the course that was located in the west wing of Charles Rennie Mackintosh's Glasgow School of Art. And what a privilege it was to be a student in such a building, working in the great north-facing studio or just generally mooching about in its richly detailed corners or sitting with a book in the 'hen-run' or the library, the building's *pièce de résistance*.

The first Principal of the Glasgow School of Architecture was a Frenchman, Eugene Bourdon, who introduced a Beaux-Arts system of architectural education in the years before the First World War. It was strongly committed to Classicism and that legacy still prevailed 40 years later; it was quite bizarre that it should have been the educational offering in this magical place. We were taught nothing of the Modern movement or of CRM, who was one of its early stars. Instead we spent hours in esoteric studies such as sciagraphy, the study of shadows and, in our case, not any old shadows but those thrown on the Classical capitals,

Doric, Ionic and Corinthian, of ancient Athens and Rome. The film director Serge Eisenstein had a similar scholastic experience: 'drawings …. some bored caryatid, some conceited Corinthian capital or a plaster cast of Dante'. It was indeed tedious stuff, but some consolation could be found in draughtsmanship and the weighted quality of line that can be achieved with a graphite pencil, bringing to life the shadow and the geometry of an early Greek capital. It seems incredible now, when the drawing board has been overtaken by computer graphics, that we were honing our skills on cartridge and hand-made papers, traditional craft that was to generate my interest in printing and Japanese wood-block prints in particular.

Their off-centre compositions of flat plane imagery had me hooked. In looking for examples I rummaged about in antiquarian book shops and the book barrows of the streets with some success. In many cases they had been used as paper packaging for ceramics and Glasgow's seafaring trade had made it a relatively rich repository.

The geometry of perspective is an intellectual business that conditions what we actually see. Although linear perspective was known to the ancient Greeks, it is considered to be a product of the 15th-century Renaissance, and may be thought of as drawing with a single vanishing point usually on the horizon, all lines parallel with the viewer's sight-line receding to it. But another interpretation lies in Tim Robinson's *The Curvature of the Earth*, 'The trick of drawing in perspective is to imagine that one has a single, cyclopean eye…The result is nothing like the world as registered by two eyes in a mobile head and backed by an interpretive brain, but it is curiously convincing'. I do know that understanding this business can have a stultifying effect on illustrations, and mine are altogether happier when released to the crazy geometry of boats at sea. The Japanese print-makers, for whom size according to distance did not necessarily follow, used a concept of space that was perceived in concentric rather than linear perspective, with pictorial scale taking precedence over natural scale. Mackintosh's French watercolours are similar to the wood-block prints in that they present the volumes and mass of buildings, sea and rocks in flat planes, in his own quite inimitable style.

Outwith the strange world of Beaux-Arts education was another, that of the hard-headed commercial Glasgow that cared little for history or the arts or CRM, their very own local genius. I can vouch for the existence of an Ingram Street store-room, packed from floor to ceiling with Mackintosh's furnishings and glass panels, all held in chaotic profusion. No doubt there are bits and bobs of his genius, filched from this treasure trove, scattered around the globe.

But the greatest stain on the city's character had to be its notorious sectarian divide, operating quite openly in public and private life. Our family, with friends of all persuasions, was unaffected by this poison and its shadow is much diminished in the Glasgow of today. The art school on the rise of Garnethill, our very own Montmartre, was a haven free of that nonsense. There, 'The Clyde Valley Stompers', the ballads and blues of the early folk revival, along with oil paint and turps, encouraged dreams of other heard-of worlds that were in the air of its gas-lit streets, but it could not quite compensate for the outdated education on offer and by the end of my third year I was planning to move on.

Edinburgh 1956

I had on occasion been visiting Edinburgh and these visits reinforced my earlier positive impressions. It was time to make a move, although it turned out that I was too late to submit a formal application for entry to Edinburgh's School of Architecture. Undeterred, I decided on taking my chances with a visit and, armed with my folio, I arrived and asked to see Ralph Cowan, the Head of School. It was lunchtime in the summer term with no-one but a janitor around. He pointed me in the direction of the Head's office and that kindly man gave me a hearing. I had moved east. Such youthful self-confidence might occasionally pay off, but that was then, a time when a handshake could ratify a contract.

So it was that I arrived in Edinburgh with a cerebral load of Beaux-Arts baggage that included the history of classical architecture on which it was based. It was about to be shunted into a reference file at the back of my head.

The School of Architecture was attached to Edinburgh College of Art, in an environment that was liberal and benign. Technical studies, such as acoustics and structures, were carried out in Heriot Watt College, and a lively social life ticked over in Bohemian Stockbridge. The Folk Revival was all around, and working in the studio above the West Port across from the Castle on its rock, it was not unusual for a spirited rendition of *The Four Marys*, so related to that place, to gradually build from a chorus of young students. It would have pleased Joan Baez, but be inconceivable today. This package, set in this special city, provided a milieu that was quite novel. In hindsight, it triggered my application, as never before and perhaps never thereafter, to the understanding of not only the chosen subject of architecture but a host of new introductions in allied fields.

It was a mixed bag of young students from various backgrounds and faculties who would come and go through the door of the St Stephen Street basement flat in Stockbridge and it was with this circle of friends that these interests, in tandem with formal studies, developed, in a flat where Beethoven and Sibelius filled the air during waking hours. I slept on a bunk in a corner of the kitchen, below a great yellow oil painting by Rod Carmichael of a paraffin lamp, the paint still retaining its scent in that odoriferous place. I read everything that was to be read in translation of classical Russian literature and whenever I now open a page of my favourite, Turgenev, I am transported not only to the Steppe but to a seat by the Water of Leith, where I first came across his work. This reading was international in context and of such a scale that the Stockbridge years seem extended and the significance of that part of the city, where it took place, amplified. In retrospect some of it, such as the Dostoevsky, provided little profit but it was a literary exposure that informed and supported a cultural ideal that has followed me about over the years.

Although the 1960s get the blame or acclaim for the sexual revolution, the works of its main protagonist, Wilhelm Reich, were well known to us in the earlier decade. His writings were held in an 'index' in Edinburgh's Central Library and prim librarians knew we were up to little good in attempting to sign them out, but they provided some welcome understanding of the sexual repression that was the common lot of these times. In the specialist medical bookshop I found a copy of his *Mass Psychology of Fascism* that eventually went off with Jim Haynes, one of the founders of the Traverse Theatre, to Paris where he was until recently promoting that revolution. Reich's maxim, 'Love, work and knowledge are the well springs of our life. They should also govern it' still has much to recommend it.

The highlight of any visit to London in the late 1950s had to be a visit to Alec Tiranti's bookshop in Charlotte Street, the sole outlet in the UK for the wonderful *Documents of Modern Art* (Wittenborn Schultz, NY) with writings by Moholy-Nagy, Mondrian, Kandinsky and Arp from Europe, along with Chicago's hero, Louis Sullivan. Dipping into those works now, that so impressed me then, the Bauhaus fellows hold up well, while the great energy with which Sullivan promotes the case for an architecture fit for a modern world is less than easy, as it is carried on prose hooked into another time and from the same assured firmament as that of his compatriot Walt Whitman. It was Sullivan's young apprentice Frank Lloyd Wright who proceeded to say fluently what might be done and then by example did so.

On home ground, the cultural void that was left in our educations by the absence of the history and literature of our own country, was soon to be filled, part of it by the work of the poets of the 'Literary Renaissance' with whom we shared the town's bars. It was indeed an educational bonanza and it slotted well into the non-conformist lifestyles and our notions of social progress. A few years later, with more pennies in our pockets, we were regulars in the poets' pubs, The Abbotsford, Milnes and The Café Royal, along with the memorable poets of the time, and some roll of honour it was – MacDiarmid, MacCaig, Goodsir Smith, Garioch, Mackay Brown and on occasion, from the Gaelic world, Sorley MacLean and others. The event of the year with this lively bunch was the 200 Burns Club supper, the alternative to the suppers of the national Burns 'syndrome'. We would purchase tickets for this affair, which might be held in a local hotel or off we'd go in a bus from the steps of the Royal Scottish Academy to a border town, not quite sure of where we were heading. They were lively events: how could it be otherwise with Hugh MacDiarmid to the fore, and flyting – Chambers's Dictionary has it as 'a scolding match, especially as a poetical exhibition' – not unknown at, or from, the top table. And on MacDiarmid's death it was his friend Norman MacCaig who suggested, splendidly, that Scotland declare three minutes pandemonium on the anniversary of his going.

Nor was there escape from the Highland connection in Edinburgh's folk music howfs, where one could catch some startling performances, not always from a stage. I think of an occasion when I stood behind two pipers in a crowded Oxford Bar who, between drams, were considering pibroch (*piobaireachd*) at great length in flowing communication carried almost entirely in *canntaireachd*, vocables, without words, while surrounded by the normal Friday evening bedlam.

But there had to be a sober bias to my time in this cultural space and it lay with architecture, the art and science of building, which was to be the linchpin of my working life. The Glasgow School of Art interlude had provided but an introductory study of the building forms and styles of select civilisations located in the Mediterranean basin, styles that are known to us as 'classical'. Such studies were to cater for an architecture that harked back to the classical benchmark of the 15th-century Renaissance, with all notable building being dependent on wealth and power. They were concerned with but a corner of the world's building forms since man's first shelters. All the Western world's banks and most of its public buildings, including the New Town of Edinburgh, where this student was sitting, were in that style. It was the architecture favoured by the powers that be, to inspire confidence in the stability of their institutions, although surrounded, as most of it was, by the urban squalor of the Industrial Revolution. However, the banks have now all but vanished from off our streets and the Doric, Ionic and Corinthian capitals of their entrance facades greet the merry users of pretentious public houses, the new owners of these palaces being the brewers.

The writings of Louis Sullivan, Frank Lloyd Wright, Gropius's Bauhaus and others had put the ideological clutter and the anomaly of the matter of 'style' into historical context, but it was slow to disappear. The 'revolutionaries' of the Soviet Union had taken to it, and a curious grouping known as 'Postmodern' fought off its protracted demise. Prince Charles, a strange bed-fellow, piped up on occasion to complain about building form that lacked the historic impedimenta of architraves, classical colonnades and other retrospective details, perhaps in respect of his ancestors of the Stuart and Hanoverian monarchies who had introduced and promoted Roman interpretations of Greek temples.

It is with some reluctance that I turn to exhuming the dreary story of time lost to such redundant wrangles. Experience of CRM's Glasgow School of Art had convinced me of another way, which Edward Gordon Craig, from the allied world of theatre, puts rather well, 'When the imagination and the emotions can, through art, create the age, how should they stoop to mimic it?'

Whatever the quality of the imagination, it was the other world of indigenous vernacular building, the product of every society's accumulated experience, that provided a store of useful reference. There were the building types of multifarious form that provided for specific local requirements in their own traditions of construction and formed a general historic pattern, as true for the Hebridean crofter as for the African tribesman. This was a history that had been but a sideshow in our formal studies but opened more options than the earlier classical obsession. It was helped along not only by the works of architectural historians, but significantly by the works of social anthropologists, like Claude Lévi-Strauss, who was more than capable of describing how social structures in Brazil's hinterland were embodied in the physical form of their housing and how linear ornament, of a sophistication that allowed it to be read in three dimensions, was the stuff of dreams.

Moholy-Nagy, in his *The New Vision* from the early Bauhaus, reminded us that builders of much of this anonymous past were generalist in their skills, combining in one person hunter, craftsman, builder, physician, etc, and proceeded to illustrate how designers might come to terms with the machine age rather than in the opposition to it that had so exercised the artistic circle of Ruskin and Morris. The 'classical obsession' that ignored this history was snappily put down by Bernard Rudofsky in 1964: 'Skipping the first 50 centuries ... as arbitrary a way of introducing the art of building as, say, dating the birth of music with the advent of the symphony orchestra'. But the social structures that developed in conjunction with the Industrial Revolution required professional specialisms that saw the demise of that generalist tradition, although the relevance of traditional ways could always be brought back into the mix.

The New Town, now part of Edinburgh's World Heritage Site, is as good an example of Georgian Architecture as exists. It is the physical expression *par excellence* of the Age of Reason and a town as different as could be to the organic medieval one sitting on the ridge running from the Castle on its stupendous rock. I flitted about between both towns but it was the former in which I lived and worked. The hand of the Renaissance was its inspiration and it was something of a personal paradox that I so enjoyed its ambiance.

What we think of as the New Town is a town of four developments built between the last quarter of the 18th century and the first quarter of the 19th, providing commodious private houses of classical design. It was built without shops or markets, and early photographs show cheerless street scenes, rather like the joyless Sabbaths of my childhood, bereft of a populace. What a contrast from the scene that many of its new residents had left in the Old Town, that extraordinarily high tenemental town where rich and poor lived cheek-by-jowl in a vertically stratified mix, but where overcrowding and squalor had spurred the development of the other. The enormous ambition of the New Town proposal was to offer refinement of every kind, 'a city of repose, of contemplation; of learning and the arts', and in this it was successful. However, it was to see an end of the social synthesis that had been the life of the old vertical town, and the eminent philosopher David Hume was unlikely to find himself in discussion of theological issues with a fishwife on the streets of this brave new world.

The plans of the New Town's architects were, for the most part, laid out in grid form as for a flat site, although the natural terrain was anything but. The great good fortune of the New Town lay in the natural topography of its site, its conjunction to the south with the Castle rock and Old Town, and to the north with the Valley of the Water of Leith, where a mixture of late Medieval, Georgian and Victorian building would create spatial magic that swings with a twisting river and dramatically changing levels, producing two miles of townscape as rewarding as anything in my experience.

Notwithstanding the grandeur of the Georgian stone town within a town, Robert Louis Stevenson, a famous native of the place, had some words on squandering the advantages of its splendid site: 'The architect was essentially a town bird, and he laid out the modern city with a view to street scenery, and street scenery alone. The country did not enter into his plan; he had never lifted his eyes to the hills'. Well, I can see what he meant as I have only felt really comfortable in the light and airy upper floors of the 'grandeur', with the Ochil Hills and Highlands beyond the North Sea's convergence with the expansive Firth of Forth. And what of buildings that ignored other natural site conditions in their planning, paying heed to neither the path of sun or wind and dependent on blind chance to see any of the former's rays. But nothing unusual in that, as this was the norm in European city-centre development of the time, when the show of street grandeur, Haussmann's Parisian boulevards for instance, was a priority of the architect's brief. The internal planning of the New Town venture was consistent and of a piece with the external grandeur, all to layout patterns providing for the rigid 'upstairs and downstairs' social framework of 19th-century family life, that had all but gone by the end of the First World War.

This was my youthful take on the romantic city, acknowledging with some sensibility its shortcomings as a physical template for living, but with no qualms in enthusiastically celebrating RLS's 'this dream in masonry and living rock', providing as it did a backdrop conducive to the obsessive dreaming of these days.

Now it is a city visited by the multitudes, with more than two million tourists climbing annually onto the castle rock, who wander about in the alleys and wynds of the early medieval Old Town footprint, savouring the rich historical patina of its stones and a linear pattern that is conspicuously less in tune with Euclidean geometry than that of the New Town, across the valley to the north. Here it is theatrical space that wins out, over education's predilection for the literary. Just as in Paris, and notwithstanding the Villon or Voltaire that may be afloat in one's head, it is to the physical attractions, within a single kilometre and the passage of 650 years, that one turns: Sainte Chapelle, where the quality of light from its 14th-century stained glass tints the very air, and Jean Nouvel's *Institut du Monde Arabe* (1988) with its façade of photosensitive panels automatically opening and closing to the movement of sun and cloud, illuminating dramatically the glories of the ancient Arab world.

Central Europe 1957

That academic year of 1956–57 was good to me and it is pleasing to recall how its liberal education could be seen to affirm the generalist tradition of the Scottish Enlightenment, much of it happening outwith the hallowed walls of academia.

The summer term came to an end and the project that I had been working on got lucky with the adjudicators as I was awarded an Andrew Grant travelling scholarship, to be taken that summer. The project that provided this useful prize was for an interlocking housing and studio complex for painters and sculptors in the Dean Village and, had I then the experience of artists and their ways that I gained while on the board of Edinburgh's Demarco Gallery 40 years later, I doubt if I would so enthusiastically have immersed myself in the concept of such a commune. But youthful romantic notions will out, and just as I was planning the normal young architect's grand tour of the architectural splendours of Renaissance Italy with my scholarship, there was a visit to our department by a professor from Krakow. He suggested that there might be a student exchange with his department and Professor Cowan thought I would find it of interest, commenting, 'You can see Italy's treasures at your future leisure'. My knowledge of Poland was perfunctory but, as our allies in Second World War, I had a friendly regard for Poles and decided to take up the offer. I was not to regret it.

As part of the arrangement with Krakow I was to give a talk to interested students and staff on what we students of architecture were up to in the West. There were no cheap flights in those days and, in any case, the present cheap carriers would have looked askance at my load of luggage, including drawings, documents and a large reel of a film that had been made by Edinburgh students of Corbusier's *L'Habitation de Marseilles*, accompanied by the accomplished jazz of clarinettist Sandy Brown, himself a student in our department.

I set off with this lot by train, crossed to Hook of Holland and trundled across the grey North European plain to Berlin, where I planned to see Alvar Aalto's contribution to Interbau, a large post-war exhibition of architecture, featuring the work of some of the world's best-known architects. Trains did indeed trundle in those days and the drear landscape had me wondering why I had not chosen the Florence option. It was also my first experience of going through the 'Iron Curtain'; not made easy by my baggage, which was prodded by border guards and sniffed by alsatians. My college provided the travelling scholar with a document in half a dozen languages that had been penned in an earlier genteel time: 'The Town Council of the City of Edinburgh as governors of the College will deem it a favour if Officials of Customs and Passport Departments…will give the student assistance…blah, blah' and I could imagine the reception that such a document would have occasioned from these aggressive dogsbodies, who were convinced that I was carrying bullion or bundles of dollars. It did not get any easier on arrival late of an evening in Berlin, where the only student accommodation I could find was well out of the city centre. However, it proved to be a blessing, as a room was to be shared, for my week in the city, with an Egyptian student of European history. This was 1957 and Britain and France were still extricating themselves from the idiocy of their attack on Suez, so it was with some trepidation that I considered the introduction, but I needn't have worried as we shared similar views, along with rump steaks and bottles of beer most evenings of the following week. We admired the ladies of the night who paraded about in profusion on the streets of Berlin at all hours. As we were putting the world to rights, we gave them scant attention but he furnished me with a few Berliner expressions that he claimed would ease communication should an occasion arise! They still lie untranslated and unused in my head.

There were plenty of signs of the recent past on the streets but the new Kurfürstendamm's stainless steel and glass portrayed something of the polish that was to be associated with a resurgent West Germany. Alvar Aalto's apartment building at Interbau was, however, for me the real MacKay. The access to the eight-storey block was from an entrance hall with a fluid blue/black ceiling around which the structural columns danced, reminiscent of Matisse's painting *La Danse,* while the individual apartments echoed something of Aalto's interest in designing 'from the inside out', with plan forms that grouped the accommodation around a living area, extending naturally onto an open-air patio.

'Checkpoint Charlie' had not yet been invented, and when it was time to move on I had to get myself onto the S-Bahn that would get me to Friedrichstrasse Station in East Berlin and the train that would take me through East Germany into Poland. This was the generally accepted hole in the Iron Curtain between Western Allied and Soviet sectors, and I was barely convinced that my paper credentials would see me through the hostile frontiers ahead. My Egyptian friend, ever resourceful, got hold of a baker's bike with large baskets that could accommodate my baggage. We wheeled it through the city to the S-Bahn, said our farewells and wished each other luck, and off I went successfully through the barriers into the East and onto another 'trundler', being carried on tracks that just a few years earlier had carried multitudes in much more ominous transports.

If there was a pre-war Baedeker available I did not have it, and all the 'rough' guides had yet to be invented. But when planning the trip I did not think that there could be much less on offer in the way of sustenance than the MacBrayne steamer's post-war provision, with which I was accustomed back home – how wrong could one be. There was no provision of any kind on platform or train on a very slow stop-start journey to Krakow and, in my hunger, the dream of Florence was again to the fore. However, as always on such occasions up pops Lady Luck – this time in the form of a large peasant woman with two small fair-haired boys, who boarded the train somewhere between Poznan and Wroclaw and shared, from her great straw basket, their meal of pickled cucumbers and pork fat. As I was never short of paper, I entertained the boys with paper airplanes and gave them some half-crown sterling coinage, the weight of which they could not believe. Perhaps somewhere there is a pensioner Pole who, at the back of a drawer, has this memento of our meeting.

My arrival in Krakow was again in the dark of evening, but on this occasion I expected to be met by my Polish host. This did not happen and I struggled out of a dimly lit central station with my load into the equally dim street, lit by street lamps of a dark green hue. It was not at all inviting to one who possessed not a word of Polish, but I did have a scrap of paper with an address in Ulica Kielecka. There was a policeman floating about in a great-coat that took on the shade of the street-lamp and I went up to him with the scrap. He took it and, striding into the middle of the road, stopped a tramcar and spoke to the driver, who dismounted. Between them they stowed my baggage in the driver's tight compartment in the front. I was invited to join the driver and off we went for a bit before arriving at the terminus. The driver picked up half my load and motioned me to follow, leaving the tram and new passengers to await his return from delivering me to a pitch-black stair in a pitch-black street. In the circumstances I thought it mighty civil of him and well beyond the call of duty – reinforcing my view that most folk, other than border guards, are decent, even to someone who could have been from another planet in relation to our recent histories. None of these ordinary folk that I met had ever met anyone from the West.

My hosts were surprised at my unexpected arrival and, as Poles, were astonished at the helpful treatment at the hands of a policeman. There had been a mix-up between my host Andrzej Basista and me on the time of arrival, language no doubt having a hand in it, but all was well.

The Barbican in the foreground, the Florianska Gate in the background, and the tower of St. Mary's Basilica in the distance.

What a difference twelve hours can make, day from night in this case, as I strolled into the old city with Hanka, Andrzej's wife, on a morning of hazy sunlight. There was no transport to speak of, trams and a few cars but the noticeable presence of horse-drawn peasant carts on pneumatic tyres. We passed through the medieval fortifications of the Barbican and Florianska Gate into the core of the city and the first and longest-lasting impressions – masonry of delicate tapers on battered walls giving a great sense of solidity, to a large central square with St. Mary's Basilica and ornate market building, flanked by a colourful flower market run by peasant women in wellington boots and headscarves. While in the absence of traffic noise, the romantic tinkle of piano practice spilled from upper floors, and just as Paris had its scent of Gauloise, here Balkan tobacco was the prevailing aroma. The city had escaped destruction in the war and within the lines of its medieval ramparts it formed a compact unity, as yet unaffected by post-war commercial development. It was hugely atmospheric, sitting on its plateau above the Vistula, in the mild weather fluctuations of late summer / early autumn.

Here, some 500 kilometres from the sea and about as far in Europe as one can be from it, I was impressed. This was 'foreign' to a youth who had never been further than 20 miles from the shores of an ocean. I knew nothing of this impressive little city, but the physical reality bore witness to its historical significance – capital of Poland until 1609 and the major city, along with Lvov, in that complex cultural province of Galicia that straddled a number of central European countries while governed by Austria in the latter part of the Partitions of Poland that had begun in 1772.

Italian architects, at the invitation of the Jagiellonian monarchy, had great input into the formation of this city and it struck me that in the baroque churches at least, I was getting a taste of the Italian trip that might have been, but my favourite in this plethora of architectural riches was the simple Romanesque of the church of St Andrew that had survived Turkish depredations in the 12th century.

Apart from destroying part of the city's fortified wall and replacing it with a green belt (the *Planty*) the notable Viennese influence was concerned more with the civilised quality of life

– sweetmeats and music come to mind and there was a hint in all discourse with Polish friends of a nostalgia for Galicia's connection with Austro-Hungarian times, quite different from the voluble aggression towards the other two parties of the Partitions – Russia and Prussia.

Although I knew nothing of it at the time, the Scots too had been around in some numbers in this part of the world. This large migration of what we would now call economic migrants arrived via the Baltic in the 17th century, escaping from civil war and famine in Scotland. It was but one of the migrations to the Baltic States, the Low Countries and France. They were as significant in scale as the later migrations to the Americas and Australasia and it is reckoned that 30–40,000 could have been in the provinces through which the River Vistula flowed. They were a mixture of all sorts – wandering pedlars, merchants, craftsmen, professionals and men in arms. The general Polish attitude of contempt towards those involved in trade provided opportunity for these Scots, many becoming settled burgesses, organised into guilds and brotherhoods with Scottish autonomy and many privileges. In Krakow there were 'divers Scottish merchants … of singular note for honesty and wealth', wrote William Lithgow in the 1630s and 'the connection between Scotland and Poland, considering the distance and interval of nations, wonderfully intimate'.

Recently the Poles have arrived in Scotland on a scale that mirrors that economic migration in the 1600s and replicates the large Polish community that found a welcoming host in Scotland at the end of the Second World War.

But no influence of incomers can come close to that of the Jewish population, when in the 13th century and for centuries thereafter they found refuge in Poland from exclusion and pogrom elsewhere in Europe. They became the backbone of the Polish economy in medieval times and by the middle of the 16th century 75% of world Jewry lived in that country. Their quarter in Krakow was the district of Kasimierz, below the royal palace of Wawel, but now devoid of its Jewish population, the holocaust having done its deadly work. At the insistence of my host, I reluctantly made the obligatory visit to Auschwitz Concentration Camp. Although the process of sanitisation was underway, the mounds of hair, teeth, spectacles and footwear were more telling than the bricks of the remaining structures. *Arbeit Macht Frei*, (Work Makes Freedom) greeted one at the entrance gates, whereas the inmates' experience proved the reverse. Primo Levi, who was incarcerated there for eleven months and survived, records his stay in *If This is a Man*, and I cannot think of a book of which I would as readily use the term 'revere'. It is extraordinary that, having experienced arguably the worst of the 20th century's obscene events, in a century of obscenities, he is capable of writing of the experience so quietly and lucidly while articulating the scale of the horror, by paraphrasing TS Elliot's 'to efface the moment, it would be necessary to wash the wind and clean the sky'.

At the end of the Second World War, knowledge of the holocaust emerged and images of the horrors of Belsen were made known to the British public, but the shocking story receded in the following years. The horror story was shelved as West Germany was to be our ally in this less-than-brave, cold-war world, and it was 'many years before the word *Auschwitz* replaced *Belsen* as the ultimate metaphor of evil'.

The memory of this and the many other abominations that accompanied the war was fresh in 1957 and, to the outsider, there were related and noticeable population imbalances, such as so few fathers and middle-aged men in the normal social mix, but given this history, life was quite astonishingly positive and vibrant, particularly in the worlds of music, drama and the visual arts.

This new understanding of what had happened in Central Europe affected my comfortable juvenile memories of the war – my family's experience was put in perspective and diminished by the scale and enormity that had overwhelmed this place. Yet optimism was in the air in that autumn of 1957 and life was going to improve: a dream supported by the coming to power of Wladyslaw Gomulka the previous year, when he successfully stood up to Kruschev and succeeded in having Russian troops removed from Polish soil, while avoiding the bloodbath that occurred close by in Hungary in November of that year.

In the 500 kilometres from the Baltic, the great part of the Polish plain and the River Vistula rise but 200 metres. There is then a quite dramatic rise to the Czech and Slovak frontiers, formed by the western part of the Carpathian mountain chain. Andrzej and I now took off for the hills on a Vespa – south and east to the Beskid hill country of old Galicia, fringed by the ragged high tops of the Tatra range.

East of the attractive tourist areas around the skiing centre of Zakopane and the lovely limestone peaks of Trzy Korony there is a pocket of land of less than 400 square kilometres that is bounded to east and west by the mountain rivers Dunajec and Poprad, to the south by the mountain barrier, and tailing off to the north at the junction of both rivers and the town of Nowy Sacz. We skirted about both sides of this 'pocket' – an area of old spa villages and little timber churches, some glorying in ancient polychrome. This was before the flooding of the Dunajec plain, when Niedzica and other fortifications stood above fields of little stooks, reminiscent of Highland Scotland. The occasional country inn could have been compared to those that were reported by Walter Scott-inspired 19th-century tourists and their general complaint about the common fare. Probably my experience on the *Seonaid* had me take the palliasse bedding and sustenance fare in my stride, but alas not the country flea!

We wobbled about on pot-holed country roads and tracks, regularly behind peasant carts on old pneumatic tyres pulled by the ubiquitous horse. They were more elegant than the workhorses of home, due perhaps to the glory of ancient Polish arms, its cavalry, but their droppings marked the way and the notable quality of vegetable produce that graced the country's tables surely benefited from this humble harvest.

Quite by happenstance we found ourselves on a deeply rutted track that ran by a brisk stream into lightly wooded hills, the contours of which were defined by narrow agricultural terraces running parallel to the watercourse. After some miles we came upon the village of Jaworki, that was to have some future significance for me. On a rise above the stream sat the village church, an onion-domed *serkiev*, and log dwellings and their barns with steeply pitched shingle roofs were scattered about close to the stream. It was an attractive, well-tended scene: the log constructions, many caulked in pale blue, sitting on white-washed masonry bases amid a fretwork of deciduous trees in early autumn colour. We moved on and then,

Jaworki, the Greek Catholic serkiev *(Jana Chrzciciela) on its rise above the village.*

91

much to our surprise, a further mile brought us to a smaller settlement, Biala Woda, that had been burnt to the ground; quite shocking, on a golden day of early autumn in this gentle rolling hill country; and the fact that it could have happened yesterday heightened the impact. It was unlike the vestigial ruins of the Scottish 'clearances', where one comes across moss-covered ruins almost anywhere in the Highland hills. Here, the burnt timber remnants on their masonry bases and bits and bobs of domestic peasant life still littered the ground.

It turned out to be but small-scale evidence of what had been a war within a war; a ferocious internecine conflict between Polish and Ukrainian partisans that had been fought in tandem with the major event, but had continued beyond the end of the Second World War in 1945.

This area in the borderlands between Poland and Slovakia had been settled centuries earlier by a Ruthenian ethnic group of peoples known as Lemko. They were Uniate in religion since the 16th century, Roman in doctrine and Eastern Orthodox in practice, and it was their great misfortune to be considered by the Polish Government in the aftermath of the war as Ukrainian. Almost half a million Ukrainians and Lemkos from Galicia were brutally uprooted and transported to Poland's newly acquired territories in western Poland; as tit-for-tat massacre and atrocity between Poles and Ukrainians continued well into 1947.

The horror of all this had not been written up at the time, nor were Poles anxious to talk of it. There had been quite enough awfulness in every corner of these parts and there was a view that, just maybe, Gomulka's new regime would herald the emergence of a better world. We now know that 30 more years were to pass before the deadly hand of the Soviet Union was finally withdrawn and an ethnically homogeneous Poland emerged, an altogether different place to that pre-war Poland of diverse cultures and large established minorities of Germans, Jews, Ukrainians and others who were now no more.

We came out of the hill country and after a few more days in Krakow I left for the West. My experience was similar to that of Neal Ascherson, 'I was knocked out by the quality of imagination and energy and fun', although how the latter existed after such a history had me flummoxed. The experience had probably added but little to my knowledge of architecture, but it had provided more than an inkling of Central European affairs and the savagery that had only recently ceased.

Back in Edinburgh for the penultimate student year, studies were enlivened by my discovery of a particular book in the College's library. It was *Cities in Evolution* by Patrick Geddes, and in hindsight, it is quite astonishing that no lecturer had pointed us in the direction of the works of this polymath Scot, who had so much to say about matters relating to our studies. Not so very different from the indifference, or worse, to Charles Rennie Mackintosh that was so apparent in Glasgow – prophets without honour in their own country.

There are special occasions in this life when one comes across the means of better understanding complex matters, and the 'discovery' of Geddes was such a one. His work provides structures for the understanding and interpretation of environment in the synthesis of his triad

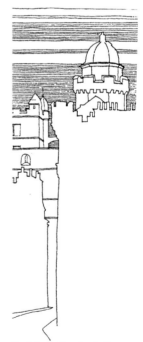

Geddes's Outlook Tower, with its Camera Obscura on Castle Hill.

PLACE – WORK – FOLK, which was assisted by, and predicated on, imagery and diagrams, invaluable in the communication of ideas. It planted the kernel of an idea in my young head that might extend my knowledge of Central Europe, located in the 'for future reference file'.

Danish Interlude 1958

Student life, in these early post-war years, was attractive. My student bursary of £190 per annum just about covered the business of living, while travel by rail and sea was inexpensive; £5, I seem to remember, for the crossing from Leith to Copenhagen on the MV *Gullfoss*, the flagship of the Iceland Shipping Company. We moved around a lot before and after graduation as it was a relatively simple matter to find employment abroad, especially in Scandinavia, where English, even then, was widely spoken and understood. Nor was it just one-way traffic, as there were always three or four Scandinavian and other nationalities in the Edinburgh classes. But now, and since the advent of cheap air-travel, EVERYONE moves around and to the furthest ends of the earth, but at what general advantage to themselves or anyone else? My travels have been paltry in relation to this travel tourism to exotic corners of the globe and my time/space perspective is closer to that of my father's twice-yearly trips from the UK to Australia on the *SS Moreton Bay* in the 1930s, when the annual mail to the Pitcairn Islanders was dropped off as she passed.

Denmark, the country where ladies smoke cigars, blazoned the travel poster of the time; well, maybe, but this little country, with a population of similar size to Scotland, was also a welcoming and pleasant place. I arrived there in the June of 1958, a little later than contemporaries from continental schools of architecture. For a week I knocked on doors of practices that already had a full complement of students, before a Danish acquaintance pointed out an advert for an architectural assistant in Odense, on the island of Funen. I made a telephone call on a Thursday and was asked to appear for interview on the following Monday morning. As I had spent my pennies slumming about for a week in Copenhagen, I went along to the docks to enquire if any coasters were planning a trip to Odense. This was in the days prior to road bridges, and there happened to be a cheese boat that was making such a trip. I had a word with the purser and was told that I could work my passage, arriving in Odense on the morning of my interview. Off we went out into the Kattegat and, rounding Zealand, proceeded to collect great roundels of cheese from islands such as Samso. My task was to roll this very smelly cargo up a gangplank and into our hold. We duly arrived around 7am on the Monday in Odense and I presented myself an hour later at the office of Vagn O Kyed. There was but minimal washing facility on the cheese boat and, as I had but the clothes that I stood in, I was aware that the condition of my attire was less than appropriate.

However, there was a short, amiable interview with the senior partner, who was smoking a cigar, which may well have moderated my personal bouquet, as I was offered the job and my cigar-smoking boss provided a key to a property where I would find a shower. All very civilised and the office procedures that followed were consistently so. We started work at 8 am and at 11.30 we were asked the smørrebrød of our choice for lunch. Two drafting tables were pulled together, a case of Tuborg was put on the table and the six of us sat down on the arrival of our smørrebrød for a quiet lunchtime chat, in English in deference to me.

This architect's practice was to illustrate simple ingenuity on the nature of the architect's drawing, as a vehicle that should illustrate and communicate information in as simple a form as possible. The vertical dimensions were always shown as datum related to structural floor levels and the horizontal always as the brick, block or panel size. One could see how the logic of this simple form had developed from the traditional Danish half-timbered form of construction and how it went hand-in-hand with the contemporary interest in factory-made components. Scotland, with its tradition in the plastic form of stonework, did not have the benefit of such an historical template; but England did, and yet, but for some isolated examples, lacked such sensible linkages in its building practice. The greed and brutal ugliness that accompanied Europe's earliest industrial revolution had seen to that.

My old boss, wreathed in cigar smoke, would have a look at what was happening in the studio, from time to time. Looking over my shoulder, and seeing that I had erased the faint pencil lines that guide the finished drawing, he remarked, 'It's better to leave these lines, as they are a reminder of how you arrived here'. Who could disagree? He must have liked my drafting, as one of my drawings adorned the office Christmas card in the next two years.

Unlike the Polish connection of the previous year, this was rewarding professional education in the here and now and was permanently to inform my own practice throughout the coming years.

Postgraduate 1959

I completed my final student year in Edinburgh with a thesis on whisky-distilling that was an exercise in building for that interesting process. It was rewarded with a Polish Government scholarship, under the auspices of the British Council, for a study of regional matters in the southern Polish hill country, quite in line with the kernel planted by my earlier visit.

My parents came through to Edinburgh for the graduation and my father and I went into Greyfriar's Bobby for a drink before the event. He was in his navy-blue serge and I had got out of my favoured moleskin pants and into a borrowed suit. I had not seen him for a year and this was the first occasion when he and I were in a bar together. We stood at the bar counter and for him I ordered a 'nip and a pony', the traditional small whisky and small draught beer in almost identical little glasses, and for myself a pint of draught heavy. Looking at my glass, he asked 'What's that?' I explained, 'A pint of local draught beer', and after a moment he said, 'It's completely out of scale with your hand'. They had what was known as a 'good eye', these old guys.

So off I went again to Central Europe. It started in Paris where I naively expected to pick up the required visas from the respective embassies of East Germany, Czechoslovakia and Poland within a couple of weeks, all as advised by their Scottish Consuls; but such a timescale was not to be and, in those far-off days before the plastic card and with severe restraints on taking sterling out of the country, I was about to become financially unstuck. The fortnight came and went while I made futile daily visits to the embassies and my funds rapidly vanished. It was a dilemma, as a return to the UK would have triggered a call-up to Aldershot Barracks. Conscription, which still had a year to run, would have seen a farewell to postgraduate dreams.

However, another dream came along to save the day. I remembered that a student friend from Bohemian Stockbridge had gone to work in Paris. HCD Rankin, known to his friends as 'Cunnie', was to become the Treasurer of the Scottish National Party, but worked at that time in the Paris office of Deloitte Haskins & Sells. I cannot think why such a name should have stuck in my head, but it did and, after some complicated exchanges by telephone, I made contact with Cunnie, who immediately offered accommodation in his tiny flat in Maisons-Laffitte in the northern suburbs of Paris. It was like being back in Stockbridge but rather more dramatic, as I slept on the floor in a canyon formed by copies of *The Scots Independent*. Long before the rise of the SNP, Cunnie was running his own modest and hospitable Scottish Consulate.

We sat up late discussing Scottish affairs and, after morning coffee, I would help remove fluff from his dark accountant's suit before we went off to the city, he to his office and myself to the repetitive round of unwelcoming East European embassies. Some three weeks later, the visas were to hand and my substantial baggage was deposited on the train in the Gare de l'Est that had in better days been known as the Orient Express. We went to a nearby restaurant for a final meal before departure. Cunnie insisted on it being rather special and that the wine should flow. The result was that I came within a hairsbreadth of missing my transport and the journey that had caused such stress; all quite ridiculous after the Parisian trials, but somehow in keeping with that 'living on the edge' of our student days. Cunnie ran alongside the departing train, throwing through the carriage window bananas and sandwiches that he had grabbed from a passing trolley… a fine fellow indeed.

There followed another seemingly interminable journey into Central Europe, to which I could have added the description 'dull', had it not been for the regular raucous visits of border guards and their dogs. I was met in Krakow by Andrzej Basista and in the following few days was introduced to the faculty members who were to become my friends over the term of my stay and beyond. They were recently qualified architects and one fine arts scholar, all of whom conveyed the same imagination, energy and fun that had so impressed me on my earlier visit.

I may have had an idea for my research project, but the logistics of its implementation were quite unclear and the lack of the Polish language a significant deficiency. It mattered little in the company of my colleagues, as we communicated freely in pidgin English and schoolboy French. Something more was required and along it came under the umbrella of the British Council in the form of the only other UK citizen that I was to meet in Krakow, Frank Tuohy, a visiting professor in the English Department of the Jagiellonian University. He was a short story writer of some distinction, who offered his staff's translation assistance.

There was to be a quite flexible pattern to my days, with the only formal requirement of my scholarship a monthly visit to report on my project's progress to a faculty professor. Otherwise I met up a couple of times a week with my buddies in their small staffroom, where Andrzej, particularly, guided me past the bureaucratic hurdles of technical matters and passes for this and that. We were always there on a Friday afternoon, when out would come a copy of the popular weekly magazine *Przekroj* (Slant) with its weekly Scottish joke, given more jocular substance by my very presence. The Poles had their own cross to bear in the stereotype of the 'dumb Polack' that had come back to them from Chicago, while the 'tight Scot' could well have emerged from the history of the 17th-century huckster pedlar in Poland. Most of that migration had come from Scotland's East Coast and the reputation of the pedlars may have returned with them to give us the Aberdonian of the Victorian music hall. But from the same stock that did come back we have such treasures as Robert Gordon's College and arguably the country's most elegant fortified house, Craigievar Castle.

I never wearied of walks around the ancient town and when I had spare zloties in my pocket I would head for the Jama Michalika café. I have sat on occasion in great cafés in Paris and Vienna but this atmospheric space was my favourite, fitted with art nouveau furnishings and stained glass, redolent of another age, and not at all surprising that it was the meeting place of *Mloda Polska*, the nationalist group which had plotted Poland's future by the end of the First World War. Here I might have a morning coffee with a slice of *Stefanka*, a firm sponge cake with thin layers of creamed chocolate, or on a bitter winter's day a shot of vodka with a plate of delicately smoked ham. And quite in tune with this quality was a refined 'old world' gentility, particularly of the older generation who had survived the Second World War, that has now gone for ever. Early in my stay, an elderly professor of architecture who spoke some English, none too common at that time in a country whose second language was French, with add-ons of German and Russian from their country's respective occupations, quite formally invited me for an early evening drink in a bar in the town's smaller square. It was an old traditional bar serving only Miod Pitny, a warmed honey liqueur, in clay jugs; and had it an equivalent in Scotland it would have been Atholl Brose served in a bothy in Blair Atholl. The liqueur had a tradition of some antiquity and the nickname of 'no-legs'. Academic formality soon gave way to a merry chat and by the time we came to leave my professor friend couldn't rise from his chair. The nickname was indeed justified, and I found myself in the awkward situation of half-carrying my distinguished new friend to a taxi.

But in between the hedonistic moments of café and bar, I developed the project and returned from time to time to Jaworki, the village that would be used as its hub. I was to investigate the regional building types and place the enquiry in a wider skeletal structure of the Place, the Folk and their Work. I decided against the conventional inventory format for the information-gathering on building forms and put together instead a system of graphic symbols or pictograms to illustrate them. They were more in keeping with Geddes's 'ideation calls for imagery … from geometry onwards', and, just as in cartography, they were more useful in the communication of such information. They provided an informative shorthand that expressed more than their own simple forms. Building types and finishes could inform their functions and age, and when plotted in relation to paths, streams, wells, shrines, etc., they gave an historic dimension to the understanding of what was going on and how major change, like the use of traditional hill-top routes, fell into disuse while routes by the streams developed.

The project became therefore a series of illustrated records, as the alternative conventional record could only have been produced with fluency in Polish and the languages of Germany,

Jaworki – the village, 1960.

Austria–Hungary and Russia, the occupying powers during the partitions of Poland from 1772 to the end of the First World War. The building study was to be a micro part of the project while the macro would be covered by more conventional mapping. Some magical discoveries popped up in the research, like coming upon an historic note that the dramatic gorge, Wawóz Homole, which rose south from the village through the Beskid hills, had been part of a caravan trail that saw amber shipped

Jaworki – the poultry have their own log cabin. The gorge of Wawoz Homole is in the background.

from the Baltic to the Adriatic in Roman times. I often sat in the sun on the heights above the gorge, musing on the atmosphere of the place, when the only other person might be a solitary shepherd. Here was a reference that gave substance to my romancing; and the quality of the mapping of this part of Galicia by the Austro-Hungarian engineers and cartographers was but another kind of revelation.

Collectivisation of farming had been turned back in the Gomulka thaw of 1956 and the life of the peasant farmer was arguably better than that of the industrial worker drafted into the post-war Stalinist proletariat. The archaic Jaworki of that time, of some 40 households spread about below its handsome *serkiev*, had an air of quiet contentment; and why not, when the natural and the man-made environments ran in such harmony. Cock-crow heralded the arrival of day and by first light the old ladies of the village were the first to be abroad on their daily mushroom searches. The scent of wood smoke filled the still air along with the calls of poultry and cattle, and the only discordant sound might come from the woodman's saw or the chains being trailed by his dray horse on its way to haul felled timber. It was quite primitive by Western standards of the time. Electric light had not yet arrived, meat was reserved for special events and feast days and the Scot who had found his native fare of 'skirlie' boring really did struggle with leaden pierogi.

Just as it was my fortune to catch the end of an era in the fishing village of home, I was now catching the end of a pastoral scene in Europe's heartland. The difference was that I was related to the former while, here in Jaworki, I was a foreigner and shared none of the peasants' history or their labours. Their experience of 'foreigners' was limited to the rampaging Wehrmacht and the liberators of the Red Army. It was not surprising therefore that they were initially wary of me, although their reserve gradually broke down in my day-to-day dealings with these naturally friendly folk.

The understanding that I may have of Tarbert, Loch Fyne, and its environs, is to do with an inheritance of birth, while here I was consciously digging into that of another community, always an exercise with limitations, but on occasion it could be enlivened by the unexpected and the incomer's fresh approach. The local may be wearied by the load or influenced by an idea of progress, just as my mother's notion that 'getting on' could best be achieved on a monolingual route, but familiarity is just as likely a culprit. Some years ago I took my ten-year-old daughter Helen for a late evening walk in the summer dark to the eastern extremity of Tarbert's Pier Road. The 'burning' was bright that night as the Loch waters crashed onto the shore and I explained the phosphorescence to her and the significance that this magic held for the traditional fisherman. She danced in her head and in the dark at such a wonderful thing and I was reminded of my own excitement at the phenomenon. Familiarity of experience may be the easiest to forget, but it surely provides the most fruitful in recall and my celebration of the natural world was again refreshed.

But if there was reservation in my relationship with the peasants in Jaworki, there was none with my colleagues in Krakow. We shared common interests in the visual arts and music and, if I had had to contend with GSA's antiquated architectural education, they were confronted by the more serious challenge of the Communist Bloc's proscription of the Modern movement and its promotion of neo-classicism, absurdly in Stalin's recent gift to Warsaw of the 'wedding cake' Palace of Culture. We would collaborate regularly on architectural competitions and with occasional success, such as that for a Travelling Theatre. The results were exhibited by the Architects' Association (SARP), and a colleague of Andrzej Basista, our group leader, phoned him from Warsaw to enquire who was the Arab, Archibaldi Macalisterski, who was working in our team. It became my by-name and was used amongst our team long after I had left Poland.

Outwith the Department of Architecture we attended the weekly performances of the Philharmonic, and there were notable ones from Oistrakh, Stern and the greatest pianist of the time, Sviatoslav Richter, amongst others. No tickets were available for the Richter, but Poles of that generation were nothing if not resourceful and even this younger generation had the 'underground' skills of their fathers, enough to forge briefs for that event. From this distance it can appear that, just as in the Stockbridge basement, we were obsessed with classical music that sat so comfortably with endless discussions on architecture. As an historic character, such as Goethe, has it, 'the tone of mind produced by architecture approaches the effect of music' and a hero of our time, Frank Lloyd Wright, 'Never miss the idea that architecture and music belong together. They are practically one'.

The 'imagination and energy and fun' that had been the experience of my earlier stay in Krakow were quite as evident now, just part of the lively cultural life of the city. Andrzej Stasiuk, writing a few years later, had this to say of the phenomena: 'In my part of the world, when times are uncertain we usually turn to culture, since it's a domain where failures are not so glaring as those of economics and politics'. But whatever the reasoning, and it is difficult to think of a period in Poland since the partitioning of the country in 1772 that was not 'uncertain', the turning to culture in the years either side of 1960 was extraordinary. I think of Kantor in theatre with his Cricot 2 offerings, the music of Penderecki among other composers, but most of all of Wajda's film trilogy of the Second World War, *A Generation* (1957) and *Kanal* and *Ashes and Diamonds*, in the following three years, which spell out the scale of heroic Polish resistance to the occupations, along with the resulting horrors. But it was not only in these elevated realms that such creativity was apparent. Poster design and graphics (the SOLIDARNOSC logo from the same stable coming along in 1980) were on the street, as also was the astonishing ingenuity of young women, in turning remnants of curtain or other sheet material into stylish and memorable garments when there was so little available in the stores.

Literary references to beautiful Polish women pop up regularly in European writing and I can quite understand why, as Krakow was graced with not a few in these years. They could be of a rather haughty demeanour, but it sat comfortably with their elegance and was quite unrelated to wealth, of which there was none. The exceptional courtesy afforded to all women was even more surprising, while the kissing of hands and clicking of heals was but part of Polish custom.

Occasionally I would break with the Krakow/Jaworki routine. While exploring the hill country of the western Beskid there was an occasion when I shared a carriage of an old puffing-billy of a train with a group of local mountain men, dressed in their traditional ornamented felt. The carriage was equipped with a wood-burning stove and a samovar. The occupants, returning to their herds, were as cheerful and colourful as the late autumn day, and as we cut into the high valley pastures they took to hanging out of the windows, letting rip with piercing whistles to which could be heard faint responses that were applauded by my new companions. It crossed my mind that D H Lawrence, whose *Sea and Sardinia* I had recently read, would have profited more in these parts in his search for the noble savage than on that rugged island, and his wife Frieda, 'the queen bee', would surely have approved of these exuberant mountain men.

What is it with hill country that breeds and encourages the wilder celebration of life? It was as apparent in my native land as here in Jaworki, where a company of local men would sit of a Sunday morning on the bridge over the Grajcarek, the best of 'babbling brooks', sharing songs and drink while their womenfolk were at their devotions. The poor quality liquor was known as Vodka Democraticzny, in disparaging reference to the Stalinist conditions of the time, and came in half-litre bottles sealed with a hot wax plug, doing its bit for the gentle revelry.

Later that year I was reminded that 'terror' could exist in the most glorious of locations. My Krakow friends, although disdainful of organised sport with its ties to the military and the communist ideal, referred enthusiastically to their two types of vacation – skiing in the High Tatra mountains and canoeing on the Mazurian lakes, and they persuaded me to join them in their late winter/ early spring skiing. I had never skied and was content to sit about with some books in the incomparable quality of air that is attendant on a world of snow and ice at high elevation. Over our evening meal they would insist that I was missing out on the finest experience and, although I was initially able to use the excuse of having no skis, the good sense of their case won the day. One of their friends, a lady called Anna who was some years our senior, was going down from our fastness to the town of Zacopane and she could take me along to get myself a set of skis. There were times when, as an architect, I might find myself on a roof inspection and, in those days before health and safety were

The chalet of Murowaniec in the High Tatra mountains (1960).

invented, I was never happy with it. I had in my mind that in this case we would be walking downhill on valley paths.

Anna, as agreed, duly knocked on my door before dawn. I followed her for some time on a slowly rising path in the snow, and dawn's first light found us on a north-running ridge with precipitous drops. Terrified as I was, I could not bring myself to ask my companion to turn around. Men were supposed to be men back in 1960 and I followed on. A morning breeze brought with it sharp ice particles from off the ridge and I wished that I was one of the 40 million flatlander Poles who were still abed on the plain that was just becoming visible as it stretched to the Baltic in the first light of morning. This trek went on for a couple of hours, that seemed like weeks to me, before we came down through afforested areas to the town. Anna suggested that we have breakfast in a milk bar, but I needed something stronger and went smartly through the swing doors of the Bristol Hotel for a couple of shots of vodka. I hired skis and took the cable car to Kasprowy Wierch,

Poland's highest peak, and slipped and slithered down the off-piste snow to the welcoming chalet, of Murowaniec, a couple of hundred metres below. Life has not been devoid of other scares, such as the failure of a boat's erratic petrol/paraffin 8hp Poppet Kelvin engine close to rocks in a heavy swell when lifting lobster pots, but nothing compares with that mountain ridge. I became quite adept on skis and Anna turned out, not surprisingly, to have been a member of a Polish climbing expedition to the Caucasus the previous year.

°°°

Frank Tuohy, in his role as a British Council professor, held occasional receptions for visiting literati and on occasion I would find myself sitting in his living room with celebrated writers like Saul Bellow and Mary McCarthy. Bellow was a small gloomy fellow who said very little, understandably perhaps in reaction to his visit to Auschwitz earlier that day, but Mary McCarthy was an altogether livelier character and aired her socialist views with some aplomb.

Although interesting, such occasions were not among the highlights of my social life. Others in humbler positions, there in Krakow and wherever I've been, have struck me as special, and gradually a chain of life-long friends was formed. One such was Andrzej Swaryeczewski, with whom I spent many Sundays. He was an architect, some ten years my senior, who had been active as a partisan, and had a bullet wound for his troubles. He knew of the Scots presence in 17th-century Poland and the museum record of artefacts, such as pistols from Doune in Perthshire. We would lunch on smoked sheep's cheese (Oscypek) and white Hungarian wine. He played guitar and we shared our native songs. From him I learned 'Deszcz, Jesienny Deszcz', (Rain, Autumn Rain) the plaintive anthem of the partisan, with a haunting melody used by Andrej Wajda in the opening frames of his wonderful film *Ashes and Diamonds*. Sunday evenings followed in the basement bars of the Old Town that hosted political cabaret, where the world was put to rights. When communication in pidgin English and Polish failed, we took to mime and paper and pencil and, when all was resolved, a bright-eyed Andrzej would let out a cry of 'Jasny' (all clear).

My last meeting with this fine fellow was accidental, but the drama rolled on. It was late in the evening and I was in a roadside shelter awaiting any kind of transport out of Krakow's industrial suburb Nowa Huta, then a notorious Stalinist foundry town. That evening it was deserted of humankind, a snowy waste swept by a wind that came howling in from the Steppe, when the call of 'hands up' came not from a cowboy but an abominable snowman emerging from the blizzard. Andrzej and I huddled together, laughing at the crazy coincidence of it and our failed attempts at trying to light a cigarette with our last two matches.

<hr />

British films of these post-war years portrayed a class-ridden society of 'stiff upper lip' types that promoted a stereotype which most Poles believed to be general and real. They were surprised that I could not begin to act the part and had little difficulty in taking to Polish ways. Frank Tuohy commented on how well-informed I appeared to be on the life of the town and how much it pleased me. He was an academic who moved in academic circles and whose short stories portray the grey world of Poland under the Soviet heel. Mine was quite another.

Frank could have acted the 'stiff upper lip' part but he would have done so with some wit. I met him one day in the town square and, as he had access to the occasional *Times* newspaper from the embassy, I enquired if there was anything eventful back yonder. 'Well, I read that a majority of Holland's population is now Catholic', and when I did not appear to consider this of much consequence he, as someone who had come from that persuasion, continued 'That means their public plumbing's buggered'. Early in 1960, a first English language edition of Boris Pasternak's novel *Dr Zhivago* to come down the same line and from first page to last I saw no sleep. It was up there with Turgenev.

Later that year my friend Andrzej Basista had a call from state security services. They required him to write a report on what I was up to. Andrzej was of a quite nervous disposition and this did nothing for his sangfroid. He was required to prepare a report and meet them the following day in the Café Literacka, with a flower in his lapel for identification…it was as corny as that. We met and concocted a story that could not possibly have fitted the lifestyle of a spy. He handed it over and that was the last he heard of them. They then visited me and I told them something of my project and off they went. It was not quite the end of such nonsense. I had a call from a Warsaw journalist who asked that we meet in the Francuski Hotel. As I was happy to have a refreshment in the up-market Francuski, I went along. But, as Frank, with his embassy connections, was more informed about such goings on, I mentioned it to him and he thought that I had taken leave of my senses, as every room in the Francuski was wired and quite notorious. Thus ended the connection with the journalist, an attractive blonde, and, in Frank's view, the likely instigator of a 'honey pot' scenario. Who knows, but there is probably a dossier of surveillance in Poland's Institute of National Remembrance, which can continue to lie there undisturbed, as I would rather retain the warm memories of my

Krakow friends than find that any one of them was coerced into concocting daft tales.

I would occasionally get caught out by my ignorance of public holidays celebrating Catholic saints' days or Russian victories in the Second World War. So it was when I went to Warsaw at the invitation of the British Embassy, where I met the Ambassador and had a chat with the Cultural Affairs officer about the postgraduate scholarship and work in Krakow and the Beskid, at the end of which he asked if there might be anything in the food or drink line that could be furnished from the Embassy shop. Well, I had taken well to Polish produce, especially the smoked meats and fermented vegetables but nary a bottle of Scotch had been seen since I left Caledonia. He suggested that I go and purchase a suitable bag, and on return, he packed it with a half-dozen bottles of Johnny Walker, the triangular form of the bottles packing well. Off I went for my train on the evening of 1st November, not realising that all Poland was on the move to visit the graves of their families, the next day being All Saints Day. It was standing room only in a cramped corridor for the overnight journey, which after a couple of hours called for some sustenance and with the aid of Johnny Walker the wobbling corridor became an altogether merrier place as we chugged into the All Saints Day gloom of that November morning. Strange that this day of remembrance of pagan origin should have vanished so completely in Scotland, while other occasions of similar origins have survived and thrive in various forms.

The stay in Poland was coming to an end and my interest in the Jaworki project taken as far as the limited resources allowed. The development of a graphic inventory, shared with students in the field, had the makings of a doctorate, but that had little attraction for me and would have required a fluency in Polish which I did not have. I felt very much at home in Poland, and had I a proper grasp of the language, I could possibly have felt even more like one of them, as the novelist John Galt's 'Men are like chameleons: they take a new colouring from the objects they are among' might well have applied.

When the time of departure arrived I chose to return to the UK by sea in the hope that I would avoid the cross-border harassment of rail travel. With the festive season in full swing in Krakow, MacAlisterski was poured onto a train heading for the port of Gdynia, by his faculty friends. A hangover was my sole problem when I boarded a coaster with a shipment of ham heading for Hull, via the Kiel Canal, and was back in Edinburgh on the 2nd January 1961.

Forty-five years were to pass before I was back in Krakow, a period that had seen the high drama of the Gorbachev – Solidarity – Pope John Paul II years and the fall of the Berlin Wall.

The core of historic Krakow had already become a polished 'open' city, smarter in all respects than what had been, but in taking so wholeheartedly to Western ways the dusty sense of its long-standing significance in the historic regions of Malopolska and Galicia had been swept aside. One may still find an old lady in welly boots in the town square's flower market but little chance of the tinkle of a piano above the babble of the tourist intrusion. In the Beskid hills Jaworki is barely recognisable. Afforestation and new housing have encroached on its meadows. The innocent visitor would never suspect the turmoil of the war years and the venomous conflict between Lemko and Polish populations in these Carpathian foothills. Only the *serkiev's* onion dome and the cemetery's early crosses bear witness to the Lemko. It is now served by a highway and a bus-park, where throngs of 'walkers' are dropped off. Dream-time in the Wawóz Homole is long gone.

But the friendships with the old faculty friends were alive and thriving in these intervening years and beyond. Andrzej Basista was a successful academic, publishing a number of important works, where on occasion he looked to Macalisterski's contribution to bi-lingual editions such as *Architektura i Wartosci* (*Architecture and Values*, 2009). Publishing for Andrzej always seemed to entail enormous last-minute efforts that reminded me of our sleepless nights before competition submissions in the Krakow of 1960. Krzysztof Brozek moved to Austria to find a better quality of work than that on offer in Krakow in the late 1960s and we met on a number of lively occasions; like Sunday in Vienna, catching some Bach in St Stephen's Cathedral before a retrospective exhibition of Egon Schiele's marvels, and then on to find the bar that Schiele was known to have used, the Kärntner Bar (1908) by Adolf Loos, the architect author of *Ornament and Crime*. The coordination of its coffered ceiling, the opulent materials and mirrored walls, effectively made his case and he would have had no complaint that evening at the 'natural' ornament provided by Hungarian lovelies who floated in and out of this jewel-box of a place. My young son at the age of six heard his father talk of Schiele's work so often, that he told his first schoolteacher that he was one of my best pals. Schiele died in 1918!

Edinburgh 1961

An active grapevine regarding work opportunity existed amongst young professionals at the time, and James Dunbar-Nasmith, for whom I had worked as a student, heard of my return and invited me to join the practice of Law and Dunbar-Nasmith. Back then Scotland closed down completely, and for days, in celebration of the New Year, and I had no opportunity to find a change of gear more suitable than the *Koszuk* (a sheep's fleece with sleeves), the moleskin pants and fur boots that had served me well in the East's severe winters. James picked me up in his car and we drove to the project in Pitlochry for a first site-meeting at the start of construction, arriving at a snow-covered site where a group of tradesmen stood warming their behinds at an open brazier. When I attempted to open the passenger door, the handle came away in my hand and James, a tall elegant figure, came around and opened the door for me to emerge, like one who had escaped from Perth's Christmas Panto, before being introduced to the gang at the brazier. They knew nothing of the reasons behind the bizarre attire and the gags kept coming until we were months into the job.

The following 15 months were shared with a cheerful group of four young architects in Law and Dunbar-Nasmith's sunlit studio in the New Town, where the partners in the adjoining room would, as the notion took them, burst into madrigal part-song that had to be a hangover from their Cambridge days, as it was hardly a part of the Scottish repertoire of the time. Like Odense, this was an architect's office with a civilised ambiance – no smørrebrød lunches, but glasses of sherry on Friday afternoons saw off the working week. And, as in Odense, I was given the keys to a flat above the office, and in spare moments of the following months I built every stick of furniture in its two rooms. Photographs of the time show something of an aesthetic influenced by things Japanese, but something of Mackintosh was also there. I ordered a grey sail-canvas, trimmed and finished to the bedroom's floor size, from an East Coast sailmaker, with close centred brass eyelets that allowed for screw-fixing through thick under-felt to the timber floor. It was a visual and tactile success… but for the little matter of its requiring to be watered from time to time, as sails do to retrieve a tight fit! None the less, I happily padded about on it in my bare feet while wondering if Charlie Mackintosh and Margaret MacDonald had done the same in their Dennistoun flat. It would no doubt have satisfied Frank Lloyd Wright's description of the traditional mat floor of the Japanese dwelling: 'A floor is to sleep on, kneel and eat from, on which to play the flute or make love'.

Aside, however, from the sensual pleasures of the floor, there were more pressing concerns for the young architect on the inadequacies of a traditional construction industry that was still, in that industrial age, based more or less on 'handicraft' skills and methodology. An alternative lay with production methods and modular coordination of building components that could facilitate construction, creative freedom unimpaired; and 13 Western nations agreed to collaborate on modular coordination in 1956. Wright had earlier commented that 'modern architecture seemed more involved with Japanese architecture than any other', and well may he have made that connection. The Japanese had, by the 14th century, a fully developed system of building elements based on a structural system and the Tatami floor mat of 3' x 6' that defined house size – the 9, 16, 36 'mat' house or whatever – providing a perfect historical example of standardisation.

Discipline and sophistication of the aesthetic is as true in those dwellings as it is in the wood block prints. What a wonder is the

Hiroshige's wood block print of a street scene, mid 19th century.

*Continuity of tradition to be seen in construction pattern, early 21st century.
(This building at Ginzan Onsen by Kengo Kuma, the architect of
the V&A, Dundee.) ©Edmund Sumner www.agefotostock.com*

holistic nature of Shinto and that culture's orderly understanding of conceptual relationships, but there was little interest in the West in such homogeneous order. A sympathetic appreciation of Japanese cultural matters was not shared by many in these days, the result no doubt of the notorious treatment of Allied prisoners in the Second World War that had ignored Geneva Convention and prisoners' rights. I had a good friend, a POW who had survived the ordeal, and he had to be restrained in their presence up until his death 40 years after the war.

If there was a cloud in the sky in these otherwise quiet times, it had to be the threat of nuclear war, as the Cold War warmed up with the US invasion of Cuba and Nikita Kruschev's support for Fidel Castro. Our jesting about red sunsets from our studio's west-facing windows, with nuclear Loch Long just over the horizon, was less than full-hearted. Bob Dylan's 'A Hard Rain's Gonna Fall' was in the making, but, like everywhere else, Scotland was birling to the folk-music revival, interspersed in my case with Charlie Parker, Thelonius Monk and other jazzmen. Amongst other arrivals from across the sea came Jim Haynes, who stayed on after serving with the US forces in Scotland, where he set up The Paperback Bookshop and Gallery and had a hand in Edinburgh's Traverse Theatre, all celebrating the alternative counter-culture of the 1960s.

Edinburgh was well served by bookshops in those days; and I think of Grants on George IV Bridge, my favourite, where one might get lost for days, as such eminences as George Bernard Shaw may have done on occasion. But Jim Haynes gave easy access to international paperbacks and if there was a book from that time that has continued to brighten my days it would have to be Sergei Eisenstein's *Film Form and The Film Sense,* an instructive discourse on how we see and represent our worlds. He saw the film medium as providing 'an international meeting place for living ideas', as interesting a proposition for those working in allied fields as it is for film buffs. The collaborative effort in the communication of ideas shines out from all his work and nowhere more so than in *Alexander Nevsky*, for which Eisenstein provides pictorial diagrams of composition and movement that are transformed by Prokofiev into the music that so enriches the pace and energy of that film.

West Africa 1962

In the winter of 1962 Edinburgh was visited by the extraordinary jazz musical *King Kong*, out of Apartheid South Africa's infamous township Sophiatown. I had heard nothing quite like it, and went around to the stage door to ask whoever fancied an extended evening to come along for a refreshment. More than a dozen of the cast came along and high above the sleeping town the music of the shebeens and the gold mines echoed out till dawn arrived. Music had some bearing on my choices in those days, and memory has it playing a greater part than money in making my world go round.

Having experienced something of four months of snow in Central European winters and being inured to the four seasons that arrived daily in my homeland, I thought the time had come to see how life might work in warmer climes. With the rhythm of 'The Gum Boot Dance' from *King Kong* still rattling about in my head, Ghana, the first black African nation to achieve independence from colonial rule, came to mind, as attractive noises were emerging from that fledgling state and there was the incentive of being able to build quicker in a warm dry place.

Within six weeks I was on the MV *Apapa*, an Elder Dempster Line mail boat out of Liverpool, heading for Takoradi to join Ghana's new national construction company; this well-appointed modern ship providing immeasurably more comfort than my earlier exposure to train travel through Europe. A thirteen-day trip, south through a lumpy Bay of Biscay that lived up to its reputation, stopping off in Las Palmas de Gran Canaria, then an elegant very Spanish little port hung with bougainvillea, its bright salt air suffused with the aroma of cigars, to which I immediately succumbed – and for the following 30 years. Then south along the west coast of Africa, through the tropic, to get the first fragrance of the continent's savannah and bush woodlands as we turned from the Atlantic along the coast just 5 degrees north of the Equator. I was reminded that the colonial past had not quite vanished when the *Apapa*'s sister ship, the MV *Accra*, blasted out 'Rule Britannia', as we passed in the ship lane outside Freetown, Sierra Leone.

The fragrance became more aromatic by the day, as savannah gave way to tropical rainforest. There was no hint that the white dots of the solitary historical structures on the palm-lined shores were the remains of some 40 or so 16th–17th-century slave forts that had served that monstrous traffic.

I was greeted on the quay at Takoradi by a tall Ghanaian with a chauffeur's cap and the keys to a beat-up Mercedes, Africa's favourite taxi. Off we went along the coast to Accra where I was introduced to the chief architect and the draughtsman, Joe Quartey, who was to be my assistant. The chauffeur and Joe were friends and, after taking me to my accommodation, suggested that I might go dancing with them that evening. Well, why not; so they picked me up in the Merc and off we went in the dark through the shanty town suburbs, stopping in the middle of nowhere, but the lights of the car picked out a circular enclosure sheeted in corrugated iron, with large white letters: 'Christmas in Egypt'. We followed the shadowy figures entering through an aperture in the corrugated sheeting of the enclosure, with tables set around a dance space and a raised bandstand, lit only by some fairy lights and candles. I was later to learn that the band, King Bruce and the Black Beats, was big in Ghana at that time and, as Joe's sister was the girlfriend of King Bruce, we got preferential treatment and a ring-side table at which cases of beer arrived from time to time. The popular current dance was the 'High-Life': basically a soft-shoe shuffle that anyone could handle. I was the only White in the place, but three or four hours later the shuffle of a couple of hundred dancers on a laterite earth floor raised enough red dust to see all of us as Apaches. A memorable night, and I had not yet been in the country 24 hours.

The professional design team of the new construction company was made up of a mixed bag of young east and west European architects and engineers, and the projects were from the whole gamut of building types required by the country's new ministries. The project briefs, as part of political/economic planning, came down to us from on high but otherwise we were allowed a free hand in the design and the actual construction overview, an attractive proposition.

In Edinburgh four years earlier, after my first visit to Poland, I joined an informal group of architects of an evening to hear what one of their number, Angus Gilmour, thought of his time at Cornell University where he had spent the recent past as the King George VI Memorial Fellowship scholar of 1956. He talked a little of Sullivan's significance in Chicago and Wright's in Wisconsin, but then pinned on the wall a couple of elevational drawings of Alvar Aalto's recently completed accommodation block at Massachusetts Institute of Technology and went on to give a detailed description of the arithmetical progressions that created the rhythm of the fenestration. It was a simple aesthetic analysis of a particular facade and refreshing indeed, after all the blethers on aesthetics that were part of our studies. He had just arrived from the States off a Cunard 'Queen' and came along to share a late-night bite at my flat. It was the start of a friendship and working relationship that lasted till his premature death in 1999. He knew of my going to Ghana and came out to join me there shortly after my arrival.

We developed a number of projects, some of which were completed on-site within 15 months, such as the large self-service restaurant for the Ministries staff, built over sheltered market accommodation, where we solved the complex planning matter of public and service access to the facilities by developing the segregated plan form of Aalto's Pension Building in Helsinki. Outwith the rainy season, the warm dry conditions helped in pushing projects along, as also did ready access to fine local tradesmen and building materials, notably sustainable hardwoods from the rain forest.

Occasionally one could be sidetracked by Kwame Nkrumah, 'The Great Leader', requiring a suitably ostentatious theatrical piece of nonsense for foreign VIPs, but such is life. In this early period of the independent state, there was little to be seen of what Franz Fanon had described as the voracious huckster mindset of emerging middle classes in the newly independent under-developed world, but there were plenty signs of Nkrumah's developing megalomania.

As much time was spent socially with my draftsman Joe and the drafting team as with my fellow ex-pats. It was difficult keeping track of relationships, as the extended

A forest of timber scaffolding festoons the new concrete construction of part of the Ministries complex in Accra.

family spoke very loosely in terms of brothers and sisters, many of whom were in fact forty-second cousins; no matter, it was a pleasant and instructive connection. From time to time I would be taken off by Joe to meet a new-born infant to such a 'sister'. In the Scots tradition I would cross its palm with silver and he would recite its lineage, just as some pals of mine from the Gaelic tradition will lyrically go back through a dozen generations.

Although Accra's only significant historical building was Christiansborg Castle, built in the latter half of the 17th century by Scandinavians and Portuguese in the exploitation of gold, ivory and slaves, there was not a hint of the colonial past in my dealings with these good people. But, on one occasion, and quite out of the blue, a German lady, a doctor, laid out the iniquities of colonialism to me as though I might have been there at the time and knew nothing of colonialism's economic and psychological degradation of subject countries. But, wearing my gentleman's

Christiansborg Castle, Accra.

hat, I let it go and said nothing to her of her nation's responsibility for the results of mass fascism in the world's recent past.

As an alternative to my weekend 'dook' in the heavy surf of the town's long beach, that was more about cooling down than swimming, I would go along to the new jetty complex at Tema where one could dive into deep water. Another party with the same idea would appear from time to time – Japanese engineers, their presence a reminder of that people's natural choice of the simple in their manner of doing the ordinary. The European would arrive with the normal paraphernalia of going for a swim – towel, swimming costume and God knows what else – while the Japanese would arrive with nothing but shorts, shirt and bandana. Off would come the shirt and bandana and in he'd go and, on return, dry himself with his bandana, wringing it out before replacing it as the smart white edging to his black mop. However, all of us were soon to give up on Tema when a local seaman reported that we were sharing its quiet deep waters with barracuda!

I cannot think of that period but another 'exotic' in social relationships, the Lebanese, appear. They were the great merchants of the coast and their food was sensationally good. Their cuisine is celebrated in the popularity of Lebanese 'hole in the wall' snack outlets wherever they appear in Europe, nowhere more obvious than in France, where something of another colonial connection comes along, on this occasion with some positive results.

My contract in Ghana was based on 15-month tours, and, intending to return after a break in Europe, I flew from Ghana; but once more that active grapevine of work opportunity at home in Scotland was to intervene.

In these pre-digital days, one's hi-fi moved around with one – ship transport was the best – and my Goldring-Lenco deck went along with a tuner/amplifier (a box of valves to the uninitiated) that my architect friend, Hamish Bremner, who had been in Army Signals at the end of the Second World War, salvaged from shipping in the breaker's yard at Inverkeithing – ingenious and good. So I had been able to listen to my vinyl collection in tropical Africa and no record saw more usage than Pablo Casal's wonderful version of the *Schumann Cello Concerto*, including his passionate introductory groans. The man and his music fascinated me. He had found refuge in Prades, on the French side of the Pyrenees, from the ravages of fascism and the Falange. Arriving in Marseilles, I went up to Prades, where he held concerts in the local church annually from 1953 to 1962, but was to miss the acclaimed performance of the *Schumann Concerto*, with Eugene Ormandy, that he gave later that year. He was not to return to his native Spain until his reburial there some years after the Spanish dictator Franco's death.

There were worthy Romanesque treasures in the surrounding mountains, notably the Abbey of St Michel de Cuxa, where the monks still talked of Casals' performance there in 1952. Then, wandering down to the sea, I came across the anchovy fishing port of Collioure and the neighbouring ferry port of Port-Vendres where, unknown to me at that time, Charles Rennie Macintosh had lived for four years until his death in 1928, after giving up on architectural practice in the UK. How strange that I should find myself in these parts, and, while on a pilgrimage to one hero, find another.

And what a place. The harbour, defined at its landward end by the massif of the Chateau des Templiers, otherwise known, and more to my liking, as the Summer Palace of the Queens of Aragon, and at the seaward end by the 13th-century lighthouse/bell-tower of Notre Dame des Anges, while between lay the beached fleet of traditional anchovy fishing boats with their high prows and intricate *flambeaux* hovering over their

The lighthouse/bell-tower of Notre Dames des Anges, a felt-tip sketch (1963) and a pencil inset of a traditional anchovy boat with flambeaux, *reminding me of tales of similar devices being used in the herring fishing on Loch Fyne.*

sterns. Mass tourism had not yet arrived and the tidy little town had retained a quiet pre-war style that many painters of the Modern movement had enjoyed and illustrated, the walls of the local hotel Les Templiers carrying work that had been exchanged for refreshment by these talented but impecunious fellows. There was still a dynamic about the place and, as I sat having a beer on the terrace of the hotel, an elderly little lady from New England commented on the paintings. The Weimar Bauhaus came up, and had she not been a friend while there, of the thinker and educator, László Moholy-Nagy, who in his

The New Vision and Abstract of an Artist provided us with a key to an understanding of spatial conception in the experience of architecture.

The significance of Mackintosh's work in watercolour was about to see the light in the following years and I returned some years later to the Roussillon to visit the places where he did his best work. His watercolour technique was not that of the controlled magic caught on damp paper, as in the master works of Arthur Melville and others, although we know from earlier works, like *Porlock Weir,* of his traditional skill with that form of the medium. But later, in *La Rue du Soleil,* the great designer portrays a moment in the movement of harbour waters with striated reflection of rich invention, in its own way an exposé of the fractal geometry of nature, Hokusai's *The Wave* being the classic example. And there is plenty of invention again, as he quietly exposes volume and structure in images of rock and masonry from around the Roussillon – what a guy.

Edinburgh 1963

But I was soon to leave the shadow of the Queens of Aragon, as a note from Hamish, my hi-fi adviser, suggested that I get back to Edinburgh to discuss an offer from a major building contractor seeking design guidance on construction systems for housing. I did just that and we agreed to provide that service with a hand-picked team of five, including Angus, back from Ghana.

Modular coordinated layouts and templates for various housing types, including two-storey terraces and complexes of broad- and narrow-frontage flatted developments, were in the mix that we developed. And although it was a useful experience of the commercial world, the inherent disadvantage of the architect being employed by a contractor soon emerged. The employer, no matter how well-intentioned, was motivated primarily by profit, and we, although requiring to turn a coin, were in the business of understanding how best to provide for social needs in inventive constructions. The relationship did not allow for direct communication with client bodies when relevant matters, such as issues of public and private space, could have been aired. It furthered the persistent idea that I should be doing my own thing, however unlikely without capital or bank support.

On a drive from Tarbert I passed a construction site between the road and the loch at the village of Furnace. Three sturdy fellows were building a log cabin and, stopping, I made their acquaintance – two of them were amateur wrestling champions and the other tried to keep up, in the hefting of long lengths of log about the site. They were building to a

Norwegian system that used spruce, but the corner junctions, even at first sight, did not look as though they would provide much protection from wind-blown rain across the nearby loch. So I chewed the cud while driving back to Edinburgh, and decided that a junction-design, better able to resist the Scottish weather, should be developed, using local redwood that was only being used for pit props. A market for such buildings in the emerging ski developments was recognised, so out came all the notes on traditional log construction in Poland and Scandinavia, while a forester friend investigated the availability of redwood from the Seafield Estates. We worked on the fine detailing of a right-angle interlocking log junction and, when we had satisfied ourselves that we had one to resist the worst of Scottish weather, a Dundee carpentry firm was invited to produce steel cutter heads. A sample junction was fabricated and an international patent taken out to protect our detail.

I went along to the Scottish agent of the Norwegian log system, a ship's chandler in Leith, in the hope that they might see advantage in our product and its being manufactured locally. The meeting proved to be enlightening on the vagaries of the commercial world, as the agent, although impressed by the log presentation, explained that he was quite comfortable with his risk-free role in promoting and selling Norwegian logs. Sitting at a large round table in his office, he went on to tell me of a time, a few years earlier, when his father had been a promoter of football pools, that most popular gambling form in the post-war years. On a Saturday evening, after the matches, a mountain of money was piled on the round table. His old father would appear, walk around it a couple of times, and, taking his walking stick down through a portion of the mound, pronounce, 'We'll gie them that this week'.

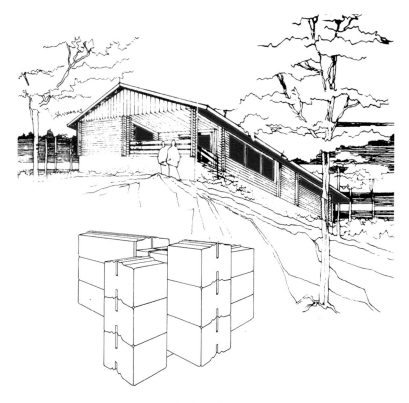

The interlocking log junction.

Another table with an equally droll connection to dollops of cash came to mind, that of the 'Wheck', Tarbert's Saturday ritual of sharing the proceeds from the week's herring catch. The crew would congregate in one of the public houses and trays of 'goldies' (whiskies) would appear. The skipper, sitting with a mound of money in front of him, would solemnly pass to each crewman at the table a pound note with 'Wan for you and wan for you and wan ...' until the mound was gone. On one occasion a relative of the skipper's wife, a banker on holiday, was invited to join the table to see how the traditional sharing process took place. When the skipper's process reached its conclusion, he turned to the skipper and suggested that there might be another way of conducting the share. He proceeded to collect in all the distributed cash, counted it rapidly and, having made bundles of the various shares, distributed them around the table, an efficient alternative sharing that had taken no time at all. But the skipper thought otherwise, again collected in all the banker's distributed allotments with 'That's no the wey we do it here', before reverting to 'Wan for you and wan for you and wan...' from the new mound. Tradition had been preserved with that prolonged process which was better suited to the relaxed social occasion that was the 'wheck'.

The Leith promotion had been but a minor setback for the 'logs', as a successful entrepreneur appeared on the northern horizon. He was Frank Thomson, the owner of the new Invergordon Distillery, with a policy of supporting small-scale industrial opportunities, and he took to the log idea from its first presentation. A Scottish log construction company, with rights to the use of the patented system, would be formed. I was to provide the architect's services and, with this cushion providing a modicum of financial security, I set up a practice, naming it 'System Design', a descriptive title that fitted and allowed for wider construction interests than that of the humble log.

The timing of some financial security was fortuitous, as a family of three daughters was soon to complement my marriage to Maureen, a girlfriend from school days. Quiet domesticity had caught up with me and for some years it was pleasant enough, but like so many early relationships it was to run out of 'pech'. Maureen was a fine mother to the girls for the rest of her life, while for me, a new family, a son and another daughter, was to arrive with marriage to Dorothy. I was now father to a family of five and in a partnership with Dorothy that has flourished ever since.

For all that I had chosen an urban life, there is no place on earth that I would rather be than messing about in a boat in fair weather, on the shorelines to the north and south of Tarbert. Every bight carries centuries-old names and the shore waters, having escaped the worst ravages of trawling following the demise of ring-net herring fishing, retain something of the great miscellany of life-forms that I knew as a boy, although the variety and scale of line catches are now things of the past.

My young family grew up with a version of the experience that had been mine some 30 years earlier. Each of them was introduced to the village within hours of their birth, swaddled in the traditional shawl crafted by their grandmother, and they were soon to realise that they were of this place as well as that other city life. They were soon hooked by an affinity to it, its allure playing no small part.

With Dorothy on Loch Fyne.

Our small boat, the *punt*, lay on its running mooring in the harbour and it was understood that I should be informed by our eleven-year-old son if he was thinking of taking her off, as she had always to be back on her mooring before dusk. On a sun-lit summer's evening I noticed that she was gone and there was no sign of the son. As dusk was imminent, I went to the outer edge of the harbour where it met the sea loch, and with binoculars picked out the white *punt*, but a tiny speck six miles off on the other side of the Loch at Kilfinan. She arrived back as dusk set in, the son and his pal, and a boatful of mackerel for which they obviously had a market, as they boxed them and carried them ashore. I went down to the pontoon with the intention of giving him an 'earful' for breaking the well-rehearsed rule, but, before I could utter a word, he said 'Oh Dad, you should have seen it out there – the sun was setting behind Cruachan* and a crescent moon was rising over The Sleeping Warrior*', and my anger was to vanish more quickly than what was left of the evening light.

*Cruachan – The most prominent peak to the north of Loch Fyne
*The Sleeping Warrior – The profile of the Island of Arran's mountain range

Identity

It is inconceivable that Danes, Finns, Slovaks and those from a host of other small nations, would question their identity, but the history of some three hundred years in a Union with a much larger neighbour has created such a dilemma for some of my Scottish compatriots.

A robust sense of being a Scot has always been with me. I had grown up in a family who quite obviously enjoyed being of that nationality, although little of a formal national history was known to us, let alone anything of the original arrivals, the first hunter-gatherers, or the Picts. Primary school had at least given us the heroic tales of Wallace, the Black Douglas and Bruce, but secondary education at Hutchesons was confined to a couple of hours of Robert Burns annually on the anniversary of his birth and the occasional home reader of Walter Scott. It was one of Scotland's independent schools, considered to be similar in ethos and culture to English private ('public') schools. It was not too surprising therefore that no Scottish history was taught and that we find a Secretary of State for Scotland, Malcolm Rifkind, who was educated at such a school, seeing fit to claim in 1988 that 'the whole gamut of Scottish culture came into existence in the last 40 years'. Here we have the mindset of the Unionist middle class that happily ignores the history of Scotland's arts and sciences, and its significance internationally over the centuries.

But a strong national identity did survive and was commonly held by my fellows and never more so than when it came to playing England at football. I remember even an old aunt in Oban being ecstatic when I was there with her to share our victory in 1949. Eighteen years later I was one of the forty thousand Scots who went to Wembley in 1967 to see us defeat the World Champions and thus, in Scottish minds, take their crown! My father disputed that team's greatness, claiming that the 'Wembley wizards' of the1928 Scotland victory, that he had attended from a ship in London's East India dockland, were smarter. This interest, or rather madness, in soccer, especially against the 'Auld Enemy', said something about the condition of the nation within a union with a partner ten times its size. We were lost to any world stage other than the appearances at a world cup competition every four years and it is not too surprising that the sense of identity survived to such an extent in this crazy connection.

We of that pre-war generation who had any political views, held onto something of the romantic international left, comforting in a way against England's perceived insularity, but focus on the 'national' condition was sharpened by the moves afoot for a Scottish Assembly advocated by the Kilbrandon Report of 1969, and impetus was forthcoming in the country's reaction to the election of Margaret Thatcher's Conservative Party ten years later. Attitudes were changing and I am reminded of the biennial visit of my French visitors' bemused response to the mass booing of 'God Save the Queen' at Murrayfield Stadium, at that time a bastion of Scottish conservatism. In just 20 years, the cultural mantle of 'Rule Britannia' that had engulfed Scotland since the high Victorian period was quietly slipping from off its shoulders.

On our being told by Mrs Thatcher, after the aborted devolution referendum of 1979, that there would be no home rule in her time, a meeting was called by supporters of change to the North British Hotel (The Balmoral). I went along and it was standing room only with a hugely impressive turnout, as also was the founding meeting of The Campaign for a Scottish Assembly in Trades Hall, Picardy Place. It was later to become the Campaign for a Scottish Parliament, which was to succeed in precipitating the referendum of 1997. I had spent 17 years of mid-week meetings in draughty church halls and members' kitchens that were enlivened by the interesting parties who shared the commitment.

Our kitchen was one such place and when I think of those who were there it suggests that the cultural context of the home rule issue was foremost. The piping of the youthful but extraordinarily gifted Martyn Bennett and the hoarse rendition of 'Freedom Come all Ye' by Hamish Henderson, its old author, were amongst the highlights. My daughter Rachel was word-perfect in that anthem by the age of eight and, with her friend Jenny, was belting out 'Sisters are doin' it for themselves' seated three years later on the same kitchen worktop.

The Scottish cringe had all but vanished. A host of new publications of previously unexplored times and events were providing back-up on the country's history at home and the diaspora abroad, amongst others Jim Hunter's expansive work on North America and Roger Cunningham's *Apples on the Flood* which dispels widely held views on Appalachia and its cultural stereotypes. Analysis of Scotland in a UK context came along in Tom Nairn's verso edition of *The Break-Up of Britain*. It accompanied me on a mis-judged family holiday to the Spanish sun, saving me from all the *Vivas*, and to this day sunlight is there in its pages just as 'Ukania' supplanted forever my use of United Kingdom.

Illustration

The old sawmill.

The early 1980s saw the life of our family greatly enhanced by our having our own place in Tarbert. It was however a time that saw the demise of the herring fishing and much that was related to it, in the nature of the village. I took to illustrating some of the places that were falling into disuse and about to be lost, such as the old sawmill at the head of West Loch Tarbert.

And when George Campbell Hay died in 1984, in memory of the poet's work I went back to his dynamic sea poem 'Seeker, Reaper' of which Angus Martin wrote: 'It is fundamentally a bragging celebration of a boat's life, written for the most part in muscular Scots, with Icelandic and Gaelic passages breaking into the middle of it as 'flashbacks' to a violent history. For all that it creates a virtue of exaggeration, in its essentials of detail – geography, conditions at sea, and the feature and behaviour of boats – it is altogether persuasive.'

Illustration from 'Seeker Reaper', George Campbell Hay's sea poem.
Published by Saltire Society (1988)

A number of the classic timber 'ring-netters' were still with us, as also was my great affection for them. I did not require much persuasion to illustrate these craft at sea before they passed to the breaker's yard or were disfigured with shelter decks for the prawn fishing and iron sheathing to their sides for scallop dredging, to which some of the fishing families had now reluctantly turned.

The series of watercolours, based on a simple palette of Payne's Grey, Prussian Blue and Burnt Sienna of such boats at sea, was to run with the energy and pace of the poem, laid out as a mirrored collage of image and text in the design and production of a high-quality illustrated edition for the Saltire Society, with an introduction by Angus Martin, who had recently published the definitive book on the ring-net herring fishing. With respect to George's ardent support of Scottish independence throughout his life, I was intent on the materials and the making of the book being produced entirely in Scotland.

New to the field, I was soon to realise that publishers are not in the business of assisting such idealism and, although there were individuals like Stephanie Wolfe-Murray of Canongate who encouraged the venture, it was clear that the conventional publishing path would not work. But I went ahead, designing the book's format, page by page, and then looked around for support; with some success, as Napier University agreed to set the text and the Clyde Fishermen's Association provided a subsidy. I put my hand in my pocket and, together, it was possible to see the colour production, the printing and the binding all carried out in Edinburgh. At which stage the Saltire Society agreed to take it aboard and publish a one-thousand-copy limited edition of the work. It was launched with the support of stalwarts of the Scottish cultural scene like Hamish Henderson, Margaret Bennett,

Donald Meek and Owen Dudley-Edwards. It was well received and the positive response had me thinking.

In considering the time and effort invested in the production of this illustrated book, I could not but be struck by the imbalance when it was compared to the time and effort required in the construction of even a minor building project, that passes into the public realm with barely a squeak yet requires just as much creative input as the publication. It was clear that there was much to be said for filling one's head with poesy on occasion, at the expense of damp-proof courses, and none too onerous a task when I thought of the imagery that was being thrown up in the works of favoured writers.

Such a line of thought and a move towards 'poesy' was helped along by the climate of change in the practice of architecture in the final years of the 20th century, especially in public works, which saw the end of government and local government agencies that had traditionally subcontracted building services regularly to even the smaller practices such as mine.

oooooooooooooooooooooooooooooooooooooooooooooo

There were two writers in particular, one making a name for himself in an international context and another whose work was of a local world, which on occasion transcended that description.

Kenneth White, a west-coast Scot, held the chair of Twentieth Century Poetics at the Sorbonne, although living in Brittany, and his *Letters from Gourgounel* and first collection of poetry, *Wild Coal*, came my way in the early 1980s. I took some pleasure in illustrating a poem from that collection, 'Fishing off Jura', floating an acetate copy of the poem onto the illustration as reflection of full moon, and, as it was Festival time in Edinburgh I found a Breton musician at the French

Institute who lived near Ken and would deliver a print of the work to the poet. Well, that was the idea, but a year, to the day, was to pass before I received a note from Ken, written but two hours after he received the securely rolled print from the boot of the musician's car! Our communication was to speed up somewhat in the next few years as we shared interests in the work of Patrick Geddes and Hokusai and his enthusiasm for mapping: 'If you want an initial and initiating sense of the world, what's better than a map?'.

I tend to 'ca canny' when moving to illustrate others' written work, but Ken's responses were invariably constructive. On receiving a print of mine of his 'Scotia Deserta' from the *Atlantica* collection of poems, he wrote: 'I was leafing through some of the lesser known texts of Whitman (the *Notes and Fragments*), and I came upon this : "A perfectly transparent plateglassy style…clearness, simplicity, no twistified or foggy sentences at all – the most translucent clearness without variation". I thought to myself at the time – that's what I'm after too. And it's a pretty good description of what you've done in that painting, no? I love it'. I contributed to the 1988 edition of *Autrement Ecosse (Pierre Vent et Lumiere)* that Ken edited, and knowing of my schematics on Edinburgh and Geddes he was interested in using that form, inviting me to have a crack at a large one, his *L'Autoroute de L'Occident, et Les Pointes de Départ Geopoetiques*. Big subject matter that worked out fine and in Ken's words, 'showing the break-off into the geopoetic field' while linking with the International Institute of Geopoetics that he set up in 1989. His essay on Geddes in *On Scottish Ground* sheds much light on the 'synthesising generalist', which was Geddes's own description of what he was about, and how his work related to Geopoetics, the Scottish Centre being set up by another good friend, the

Illustration, Kenneth White's poem, 'Fishing off Jura'.

Fishing off Jura

White moon in your light
the sea is the ghost of the land
an unholy ghost
and full of red fish of poetry
the engine throbs gently
we're out by the Paps
that gleam in the winter snow
and Mary is in her bed
miles away on shore
an unbalanced bed unlike mine
that balances the world
it's the early morning
Scotland an echo all around me
the two of us here in the wheelhouse
do not speak
for we are one man only
and save our breadth for our porridge
the thinking is a wave-word thinking
and the hands are on the wheel
ay the wheel of the world
and the poetry is swimming
red in the depths of the sea
the deep-down poetry I trade my life for
and I feel it as I feel my blood
and the land I live in
this is the place now
slacken and close
and the nets go wavering down
as the first grey hairs of daylight
appear in the sky
wait while they drift
drift
in the red and black world
wait smoking
humming a tune
as the nets grow thicker and bulge
then haul
haul yourself in
haul in the writhing mass of your whiteness
and dump your death in the hold
and then turn back
the engine gently throbbing
past the paps
towards the shore
to a morning grey as an old man
to a village
bent as an old crone
and take the path again home
to Mary and your porridge

'The Old Boat'.

The Old Boat

(For Archie MacAlister, with apologies)

The old boat is fast asleep
and the sea cannot wake her.
The sea purrs and licks her,
or roars and lashes at her,
rattles her with hurtled rocks,
scours her skin with milling sand,
and crusts her scars with salt;
but the old boat is asleep.

Nothing could wake her now:
not the hand of her absent master
alive again on the swing of the tiller;
or the protest of an oar
thrusting in the patient rowlock;
or the shock of a scrap of sail
as the wind possess it.

Sleep is a kindness to the old boat.
Her bed is the shifting gravel,
and her bones will make the fires
of men who come and and cannot
spare her simple dreams.

Angus Martin

late Tony McManus, in 1995. However, I was to concern myself more with the empathy that I felt for man's mark on the bit of earth that I knew, rather than the altogether grander but worthy aspirations of the international institute.

For some 34 years I have enjoyed a lively correspondence with Angus Martin, who has been my point of reference on matters relating to Tarbert's important part in the development of herring fishing, his *The Ring-Net Fishermen* being the authoritative book on the subject. But wearing another hat, he has become the chronicler of Kintyre's past and present in poetry and prose, and, unlike the working connection with Ken, where I might develop imagery related to his work, I would in Angus's case let him have a sketch of a subject that interested me, on which he might choose to have his say.

I came across a ruined *punt* sitting on a shore close to a worse-for-wear boathouse at the top of the Kilbrannan Sound and was taken with the juxtaposition of the curvilinear form of the *punt* to the repetitive vertical pattern of the boathouse, enhanced by the dual imagery reflected in a tidal pool.

Along with the sketch, my note to Angus simply said, 'Such craft had more interest for our forebears than the roofs over their heads'; and his 'The Old Boat' then conjured up its dramatic life and likely demise.

This West Highland interest brought the commission from the Scottish Post Office Board to mark the centenary of the Crofters Holdings (Scotland) Act 1886. Six works were to illustrate something of the lives of the crofter counties.

Morning in Wester Ross.
From series Crofters Holdings (Scotland) Act

There was, however, another side to this interest in illustration. A simple introspective meander tells me that I have been smitten since boyhood by the order of things. Fibonacci was an early hero who brought such insights, then to be joined by another in Linnaeus with the classification that made sense of romantic botany. It is perhaps not too far-fetched to see something of a link to an inheritance from a family of seamen and the order required aboard every sailing craft. But to the fore was the boy's enthusiasm for simple map-making that posed the rhetorical question: what can be made of the world around us without recourse to a bird's-eye view of the natural order of geographic form in one's head? It was early visual thinking and would develop into the enquiry of pictorial space, which accompanied every project in a lifetime of building, the architect's drawing being but a diagram that provides understanding of that physical reality.

At its most ordinary, the diagram or schematic is the doodle on the back of an envelope that saves a hundred words, but at its most sophisticated it is 'Envisioning Information' that may reveal treasures rich in meaning. My enthusiasm for the use of imagery in the collection of information must go back to the early story maps and the interest in cartography with which it ran parallel. Now I relish the simple map by a retired fisherman, Duncan MacDougall,

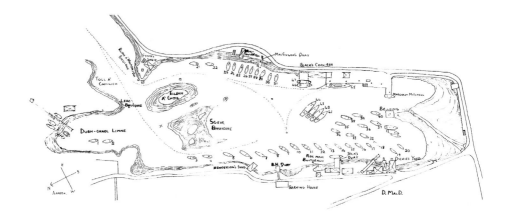

Duncan MacDougall's map of Tarbert Harbour c.1925.

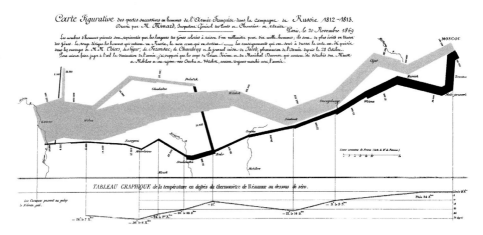

Charles Joseph Minard, *Tableaux Gra-phiques et Cartes Figuratives de M. Minard*, 1845–1869, a portfolio of his work held by the Bibliothèque de l'École Nationale des Ponts et Chaussées, Paris.

Charles Joseph Minard's map of Napoleon's invasion and retreat from Russia, with prevailing conditions, (1812–13).

of fishing skiffs in Tarbert harbour in 1925, that is as informative in its limited ambition as the incomparable map of the French Engineer Charles Minard, illustrating on a two-dimensional scale plan, the conditions and the magnitude of the fate of Napoleon's army in the invasion and retreat from Russia. The French scientist, Etienne-Jules Marey, expresses his wonder of it, 'It defies the pen of the historian in its brutal eloquence'; and I have an old copy of it clipped into a copy of Tolstoy's *War and Peace* as epilogue.

Patrick Geddes's 'Ideation calls for imagery and this in every science' had encouraged my use of schematics that were useful in survey work in Poland's Beskid hill country. His interpretation of Edinburgh's city core, with the drawings of architect Frank Mears, prompted me to put together a series of images on the city's historical evolution. It was simpler and less picturesque, but capable of expressing succinctly, something of the dynamic in the juxtaposition of the old and new towns. And I cannot take leave of the great 'visual thinker' without mention of his valley section, human landscape from river source to sea, which Geddes saw as the characteristic geographic unit that could provide 'a convenient mental picture … for much of our familiar world'. From it, 'We can discover that the kind of place and the kind of work done in it deeply determine the ways and the institutions of its people'. But times have changed significantly, and the stable communities to which he refers are now a thing of the past; one is as likely to find an accountant sitting on the hill as a shepherd or a woodsman! But the proposition was still relevant when I first came across it and produced an upgrade of the original diagram of the work – of folk in their natural habitat along with their parallel urban manifestations.

Schematics of the Middle Ages

*Diagrams which capture physical implications of place
while probing more obvious aspects of its nature*

Schematics of Enlightment

See also Appendix A.

Collaborations

In 1985 I was invited by a solicitor who was secretary of the Richard Demarco Gallery in Edinburgh to join the board. He explained that it might be useful to have someone with practical good sense on the board, as he was having to deal with a surfeit of practising artists, and his experience of the organisational abilities of the practising architect had been positive. His flattery won out.

The gallery had some fine exhibitions in the 1980s but it bounced along precariously, dependent on Scottish Arts Council grants and general good will, not least by property leases from Edinburgh Council, which provided the unused Blackfriars Church to house the gallery of that time. Erratic happenings were so commonplace that one might easily fall into considering them as just the way things should be – Richard Demarco and Robert O'Driscoll, the editor of *The Celtic Consciousness*, fresh off a plane from Montreal, arrive at my place in Argyll at two in the morning for a meeting, before leaving to get to St Andrews on the other side of Scotland by noon! Board members who would be expected to consider the director's proposals with professional competence and some caution, left these at the door as the occasional exotic ambience of the place got to them. They reverted to the slightly crazed bohemianism of student days, which was certainly consistent with the chaos that enveloped the gallery's Heriots festival during the Edinburgh Festival of 1986, as it attempted to be a funfair, a trade fair and the best of the Fringe all in one. The fairs did not work and the mediocre arts programme was poorly attended, except for a classical

Fringe sensation in Brecht's *Baal* by a Slovenian company, which failed to get a licence and was closed by the authorities for a variety of safety issues. However, the Slovenes were happy, as Channel 4 and the BBC had filmed it and their reputation was made, as also was Richard Demarco in his festival role as an anti-censorship spokesperson.

Although there was a prevailing zany context to the running of the gallery, there was the occasional production of high quality, and none more so than those arranged by Kevin Anderson in the property's exceptional performance space. As the manager of three music groups, Orkistra, The Edinburgh Quartet and Paragon, which between them covered small-scale classical music, he had agreed that there could be useful collaboration with the gallery, and with his management skills assisted in various gallery projects. However, attempts at implementing this were confronted by the director's difficulty in agreeing to anyone's decision-making but his own. It gave rise to tensions within the organisation and when the board was weighted to decide that Kevin's efforts might be of dubious value to the gallery, I decided that enough was enough.

During the making of *Seeker, Reaper*, it had been in my mind to have music and recitation as accompaniments to the poem, an idea encouraged by Kevin, whose friend, the lutenist Francis Cowan, was invited to consider the music, and Tom Fleming the recitation. After a number of sessions in 1990, we had a CD with which we were all satisfied – the rich Scots base-baritone of Tom Fleming in Francis Cowan's soundtrack that mixed bird song of Puffins and Arctic Terns with various stringed instruments to great effect. With shared interests in the cultural histories of Scotland and Ireland and their connections with others on the Atlantic fringe, we had been mulling over the possibility of collaborations since we met in 1986. We

*Cellular structure in
Gleann Mor, St Kilda.*

thought of it as 'From the Edge', calling it just that, and with *Seeker, Reaper* we had a project that was a comfortable fit, while others followed on from visits to Brittany and Ireland. Assistance from the Scottish Arts Council allowed the project to tour as a series of multi-media collaborations of musical sets of visual explorations, within separate interlocking spaces, with a nod to the ancient cellular structure of Gleann Mor on St Kilda.

Experience

The architect's practice rolled along with the years, building for both public and private clients. However, my favoured work has always been with the human dwelling place, the clientele varying greatly in their requirements and their wealth. Some of them were very wealthy indeed, and it has not been my experience that their wealth was the result of any great good sense, but more often the result of inheritance or the single-minded accumulation of more loot, at the expense of any other understandings. Having almost completed a summer house for such a fellow, he told me that it should have been larger, and when I reminded him that it would be used but for three months of the year, yet was four times larger than a normal family dwelling, he responded with: 'But you forget that I am a very big man', although he was but 5'6" if he was an inch! And another, when I had taken a commission from the wife of a couple and he, a London stockbroker, turned out to wear jackboots and was amused that his Alsatian dog would chase and nip the postman. Thankfully Frank Thomson, who may have fitted the wealth category, was not of that ilk.

Notwithstanding the sometime whimsical nature of architect/client relationships, it was on occasion possible to create a harmonious entity, intimately related to the nature of the place and the individual needs of the user. But looking back on a long career of designing buildings, I think often of the much-vaunted significance of 'experience' in our working lives; and while one may appreciate the ease that it can bring to technical and practical matters, experience itself tells me that it does less than enhance expectations in the creative process. Harsh economics and complex matters of current taste see to it that much of this experience runs with the overtly cautious and the negative, of which the youth, as inventive and creative as his elder doppelgänger, has seen little.

Two dwelling-house projects set in Highland Scotland, in a period spanning 30 years, provide an example of a disparity in the considerations that governed their design and construction.

The first, at Balnabruach, Loch Tummel in 1968, was much influenced by a passionate youthful interest in the work of Frank Lloyd Wright, especially the delightful humane spaces of his Usonian houses.

It is located on a site of birch woodland, high above a fresh-water loch, with outstanding views to south and west. The Gaelic name Balnabruach accurately describes its origins – 'the settlement on the steep'. This is rough hill country and blank masonry shields the property from the worst of the north wind, while the fenestration opens it up to the delights of land and seascape to the south and west.

Construction is based on a 1.2m structural module and increments of that dimension, which provide a spatial pattern to the progression through the house. The open-plan public space is enlivened by a floor-level change that

House from across Loch Tummel.

mirrors the clerestory roof above. It was a quite purist approach that saw it designed and built – the structure being of concrete and timber, with steel restricted to fixings. The delicately detailed design took considerable time, that would certainly have been improved on by our doppelgänger had he been around to share the youthful passion.

The second, at Garve in 1997, was further to the north, in traditional hill-farm country. It was typical of the small farmer's dwelling and, just as a child's drawing might illustrate a home,

House at Garve, from the south.

House with evening sun on Ben Wyvis.

being bilaterally symmetrical with a central front access door and windows as eyes on the world to each side. It was of slate roof and thick stone walls and situated, most unusually in these parts, on top of a rise and quite exposed to all weathers. The client required an upgraded and extended property within the same footprint.

My youthful self would probably have advised that it be demolished and that we should build anew on the leeward side of the hill. This did not happen, as, in my doppelgänger role, I felt that there might be insufficient years left to me for the persuasive discourse with my client and I proceeded, therefore, with the improvement of what was there.

The roof was removed, the wall-heads heightened to accommodate a mezzanine floor and an expansive new roof. The structure of roof and mezzanine are exposed to provide a simple structural rhythm, while the wide roof overhangs provide sheltered viewing of the southern strath and comfort to summer swallows.

Two quite different design solutions to domestic projects in not dissimilar locations, tempered I believe by the years…

Such reflections on the experience of how design decisions are arrived at may be coloured by the user's experience of the built reality, and perhaps less prosaically when Seamus Heaney gives us: 'as buildings take us in physically, we take them in, and over time they become part of how we experience, know, remember and explain … the writing, so to speak, is in the wall'.

Close

Closing on this narrative, and mindful of the Preface's intentions, I find there something of a sober tone related, I suspect, to that caution of professional jottings for building projects that I have been anxious to avoid. But thankfully it appears to dwindle as I distance myself from the world of damp-proof courses.

Except for the joyless adolescent post-war years, it has provided a pleasant jaunt through memory. 'Closure', however, does not come easy, unlike works of illustration or the drawings that allow and inform a building's construction as they confidently rolled off the drawing board. I have been tempted to alter or expand the written work at every stage rather than kiss it farewell.

But, like everyone who has written a memoir, I have from time to time questioned the accuracy of what is there, in recall. I am happy that I have not been deluded by time, in the form and content of the narrative. It should pass muster, and I would leave the persistent 'recall' concern to William Maxwell, who takes a chirpy swipe at all of us in the final sentence of this paragraph from his novel, *So Long, See You Tomorrow*: 'What we, or at any rate what I, refer to confidently as memory – meaning a moment, a scene, a fact that has been subjected to a fixative and thereby rescued from oblivion – is really a form of storytelling that goes on continually in the mind and often changes with the telling. Too many conflicting emotional interests are involved for life ever to be wholly acceptable and possibly it is the work of the storyteller to rearrange things so that they conform to this end. In any case, in talking about the past we lie with every breath we draw.'

But, for all that good sense, I would choose to find myself in the comfortable and romantic camp of his compatriot Tom Waits with: 'It's memories that I'm stealing but you're innocent when you dream'.

Appendices

Appendix A

Development of Patrick Gedde's 'notation of life' diagrams (schematic examples)

Appendix B

Examples from the architect's work

B1   Dwelling house at Balnabruach (1967)
B2   Communications Centre, Fettes (1983)
B3   St. Helen's ATC (1988)
B4   Two examples from various types of Feasibility and Appraisal studies.

Appendix A

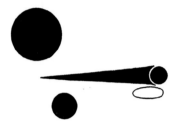

Schematics of Natural Topography

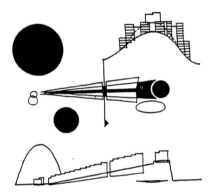

Schematics of the Medieval

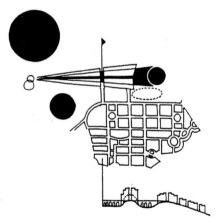

*Schematics of the Medieval and Enlightenment
(Edinburgh)*

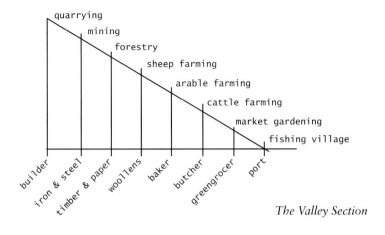

The Valley Section

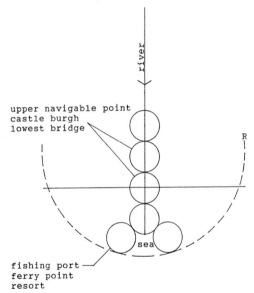

The Valley Region

Schematic examples from a study of the graphic representation of thought, in the development of Patrick Gedde's 'Notation of Life' diagrams. It also provides a numerical classification, colour-coded three primary elements (Place, Work, Folk) taking primary colours and the inter-related elements, their derivitives.

Appendix B

B1   Dwelling house at Balnabruach (1967)

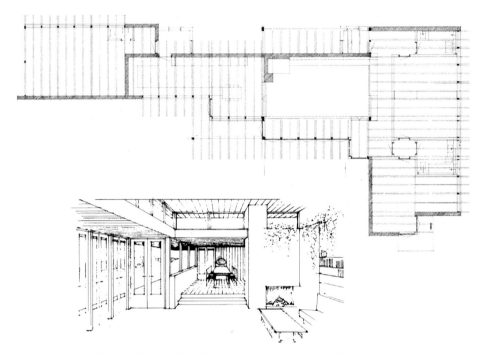

Floor plan and sketch of interior (prospect to the south-west)

South elevation (50 years later)

B2 Communications Centre, Lothian and Borders Police HQ (1983)

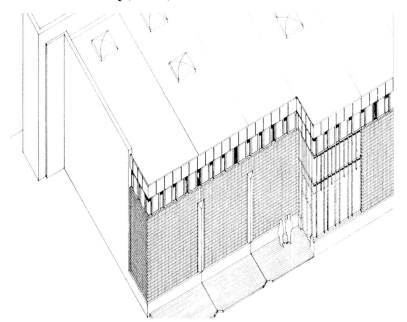

Isometric sketch

As built

B3   St. Helens ATC, Edinburgh (1988)

Providing accommodation for the eduction and care of young adults, photograph as built

B4 Two examples from various types of Feasibility and Appraisal studies.

Museum of Scotland (1984)
Investment Appraisal

Italian Cultural Institute (1992)
Feasibility Study

The Book Shelf

It provides reference to some works that have informed and encouraged my interests and enthusiasms. It is an eclectic collection of sources; many of which, like Ivan Turgenev's character Bazarov in *Fathers and Sons* and Henri Poincaré's thoughts on 'The Collection of Facts' in *Science and Method*, have moved around with me throughout adult life.

Author	Title	Publisher
Alexander, C	*Notes on the Synthesis of Form*	Harvard Paperback
Ascherson, N	*Games with Shadows*	Radius
Brody, H	*Maps and Dreams*	Pantheon
Berger, J	*Pig Earth*	Chatto
Byrne, K	*Colkitto*	House of Lochar
Buchanan, W	*Macintosh's Masterwork*	Richard Drew
Chapman, M	*The Gaelic Vision in Scottish Culture*	McGill-Queen's University
Conrad, J	*Youth: A Narrative*	Wordsworth
Craig, E G	*Index to the Story of My Days*	Hulton
Cunningham, R	*Apples on the Flood*	Tennessee
Davidson, P	*The Idea of North*	Reaktion Books
De Ventos, X R	*The Hispanic Labyrinth*	Transaction
Eisenstein, S	*Film Form and the Film Sense*	Meridian Books
Fanon, F	*The Wretched of the Earth*	Penguin
Fife, H	*Warriors and Guardians*	Argyll
Fleig, K	*Alvar Aalto*	Tiranti
Fowler, J	*Landscapes and Lives*	Canongate
Friel, B	*Selected Plays / Translations*	Faber and Faber
Geddes, P	*Cities in Evolution*	Williams and Norgate
Gibson, I	*The Assassination of Federico Garcia Lorca*	Penguin
Gowrie	*Off the Chain*	Palmer and Howe
Gramsci, A	*Prison Letters*	Zwan
Hay, G C	*Wind on Loch Fyne*	Oliver and Boyd
Henderson, H	*Alias MacAlias*	Polygon
Hunter, J	*A Dance called America*	Mainstream
Jackson, A	*The Symbol Stones of Scotland*	Orkney Press
Kandinsky, W	*Concerning the Spiritual in Art*	Wittenborn Schultz
Kay, B, and Maclean, C	*Knee Deep in Claret*	Mainstream
Klee, P	*Pedagogical Sketchbook*	Faber

Lawrence, D H	*Sea and Sardinia*	Olive Press
Lévi-Strauss, C	*Tristes Tropiques*	Penguin
Levi, P	*If This is a Man, The Truce*	Abacus
Lopez, B	*Arctic Dreams*	Picador
Lowe, K	*Savage Continent*	Penguin Viking
Mandelbrot, B B	*The Fractal Geometry of Nature*	Freeman
Marcuse, H	*One Dimensional Man*	Sphere
Martin, A	*The Ring-Net Fishermen*	John Donald
MacInnes, J	*Duthchas, Selected Essays*	Birlinn
Mackenzie, R E	*A Search for Scotland*	Collins
McPhee, J	*The Crofter and the Laird*	House of Lochar
McNeill, P, Nicholson, R	*Historical Atlas of Scotland*	Conference of Scottish Medievalists
Misc. Authors	*Ireland's Field Day*	Hutchinson
Mitchell, D	*Tarbert Past and Present*	Bennett and Thomson
Moholy-Nagy, L	*The New Vision and Abstract of an Artist*	Wittenborn Schultz
Murdoch, J	*For the People's Cause*	HMSO
Nairn, T	*The Break-Up of Britain*	Verso Editions
Neill, A S	*A Dominie's Log*	Hogarth Press
Neruda, P	*Memoirs*	Penguin
O'Brien, F	*The Poor Mouth*	Picador
Poincaré, H	*Science and Method*	Dover
Purser, J	*Scotland's Music*	Mainstream
Robertson, P and Long, P	*Charles Rennie Mackintosh in France*	N.G.S.
Robinson, T	*My Time in Space*	Lilliput
Rudofsky, B	*Architecture without Architects*	Academy
Schiele, E	*Drawings and Watercolours*	Thames and Hudson
Scott, G	*The Architecture of Humanism*	University Paperbacks
Sergeant, J	*Usonian Houses*	Whitney
Stasiuk, A	*Fado*	Dalkey Archive
Steuart, A F	*Scots in Poland*	Scottish Historical Society
Stevens, P R	*Patterns in Nature*	Penguin
Stevenson, R L	*Edinburgh, Picturesque Notes*	Pallas Editions
Stewart, B	*A Guide to Japanese Prints*	Dover
Sullivan, L H	*Kindergarten Chats*	Wittenborn Schultz
Thompson, D	*On Growth and Form*	Cambridge University Press
Tufte, E R	*Envisioning Information*	Graphics Press
Tuohy, F	*The Collected Stories*	Penguin
Turgenev, I	*Fathers and Sons*	Oxford World's Classics
Van Gogh, V	*The Letters*	Penguin Classics
White, K	*On Scottish Ground*	Polygon

171

Acknowledgements

My sincere thanks to all who have contributed towards seeing this book into print.

I am most grateful to Angus Martin, not only for the references to ring-net herring-fishing on Loch Fyne, but for his constructive comments and invaluable contribution in checking grammar and punctuation, with which I can be somewhat cavalier. His corrections have brought something of my errant school days to mind.

My daughter Anne and Heather Macpherson of Raspberry Creative Type have brought a delicate touch and refined design decision-making to the settings of text and image.

To special friends – Margaret Bennett, who has been supportive since my first jottings, to Kevin Anderson, who has, with his normal good humour, helped clarify my thinking at times and while advising on the tedious matter of copyright checks, and to Ewen Forsyth for expert photographic advice.

Grateful acknowledgement is made to the following for the reprinting of previously published material:

Kist Magazine (The Natural History and Antiquarian Society of Mid-Argyll) for the Plan of Tarbert Harbour c.1925 by Duncan MacDougall.

Biblioteque de l'Ecole Nationale des Ponts et Chaussees, Paris for the Figurative Map by Charles Joseph Minard of Napoleon's invasion of and retreat from Russia, 1812-13.

Angus Martin for his map of Fishermen's Place Names and my contribution to *Fish and Fisherfolk*.

Edinburgh University Press for 'The Kerry Shore' by George Campbell Hay.

Michael Rushe for the excerpt from his note in *Building Design,* on Seamus Heaney's talk to RIAI, 1986.

Malachi McCormick for his English translation of the anonymous 16th-century Irish Gaelic poem, 'Hail to your coming, O Herring'.

Hal Leonard Europe Ltd for the lyrics of 'Innocent When You Dream', words and music by Tom Waits © Copyright 1987 Jalna Music. Universal Music Pub. MGB Ltd. All rights reserved. International Copyright Secured.

©Edmund Sumner, Age Fotostock for Ginzan Onsen photograph.

and to:

Tim Robinson for his comment on perspective in 'The Curvature of the Earth' (*My Time in Space*).

Kenneth White with regard to my illustration of 'Fishing off Jura' and *Scotia Deserta*.

William Maxwell for excerpt from his novel *So Long, See You Tomorrow.*

Les Murray for a stanza from the poem 'The Gaelic Long Tunes'.

Primo Levi for his paraphrasing of the excerpt from TS Elliot's *Murder in the Cathedral.*

Many and various thanks are due to Archie Smith, and Ian MacIntyre of Tarbert, as well as Iain MacKenzie and the friends from our 'Highland Table' in Edinburgh. There has also been the supportive background interest from foreign fields – from Poland, the Basistas and Brozeks, from France, the Vaillots, Sanhes and Trayssacs, and from North America and Canada, the Parkers and the Rosenbecks. And I fear there may be others who are not mentioned here, to them my apologies. While, finally, mention is due to my family who have stoically endured my enthusiasms during the making of this book.